sugar & spice

sugar & spice

Flavor-packed dinners and desserts to crave

REMI IDOWU

Interlink Books
an imprint of Interlink Publishing Group, Inc.
Northampton, Massachusetts

Contents

06	08	12	14	16	21
Welcome	About Me	Cooking 101	Golden Goodness	Secrets to Baking like a Pro	Get Into the Book

CLASSICS WITH A TWIST

24	Italian Sausage Lasagna
25	Curried Mutton Pot Pie
31	Gochujang Chicken Kyiv
32	Not-Birria Tacos
34	Vodka & 'Nduja Rigatoni
36	Spaghetti & Lamb Harissa Meatballs
38	Roast Chicken with Rosemary Salt Potatoes & Salsa Verde
42	Braised Beef Short Ribs with Stilton Mash
44	Spicy Burnt Sausage Pasta
46	Chipotle Cream Enchiladas
49	Brown Stew Chicken
50	Macaroni Béchamel
52	Three-Cheese Mac & Cheese
54	Beef Patties
58	Honey Jalapeño Cornbread
60	Jerk Mushroom Pasta

FRIDAY NIGHT CRAVINGS

64	Mr. American Fried Chicken
66	Salt & Pepper Fries
68	Golden Arches Fish
71	Char Siu BBQ Pork
72	Cheeky Lemon & Herb Chicken
74	Cilantro Rice
75	Butter Chicken
78	Spicy Tofu Saag
79	Chicken Kebabs with Saffron Rice
82	Happy it's Friday Sesame Chicken Bites
84	Garlic Parmesan Fries
87	Mango Habanero Wings
88	Chile Cheeseburgers
90	Frying Pan Spicy Pepperoni Pizza
94	Korean Fried "Chkn" Wings
96	Carne Asada Tacos
98	Cheesy Caramelized Onion Rolls
101	Cajun Wedges
102	Sweet & Sour Paneer
104	Kimchi Fried Rice
106	Beef Chow Mein

CHILDHOOD

110   Puff Puff (Bofrot)

114   Mom's Best Jollof Rice

116   Suya Chicken

119   Corned Beef & Egg Stew

120   Groundnut Soup

122   West African Fried Rice

124   Yam & Egusi Stew

128   Okra Soup

130   Yam Porridge

131   Shito (West African Chile Oil)

132   Queeny's Meat Pies

A LITTLE SOMETHING SWEET

138   Single-Serve Brownie Pie

141   Single-Serve Cinnamon Roll

142   Cookies & Cream Mug Cake

144   Single-Serve Strawberry Crisp

146   Almond Croissant Cookies

149   No-Churn Strawberry Cheesecake Ice Cream

150   Air Fryer Cinnamon Bites

152   Caramelized Banana French Toast

154   Malted Milk Banana Pudding

156   Chocolate Chip Air Fryer Cookies

157   Raspberry & White Chocolate Cookies

160   Everything-But Cookies

162   Honeycomb & Caramelized Chocolate Cookies

165   Ultimate Speculoos White Hot Chocolate

166   Cream Cheese & Blueberry Doughnuts

168   Air Fryer Chocolate Sprinkle Doughnuts

170   Emergency Dessert Chocolate Mousse

173   Brown Butter Crispy Treats

174   Blueberry & Rosemary Muffins

DESSERTS TO IMPRESS

178   Lemon & Blueberry Streusel Cake

180   Sticky Toffee Pudding Loaf with Miso Caramel

182   Banana Bread Cinnamon Rolls

186   Cookies & Cream Cheesecake Brownies

188   Earl Grey Tres Leches Cake

190   Apple & Pear Crumble

193   Classic Lemon Loaf

194   Red Velvet & White Chocolate Muffins

196   Brown Butter Banana Bread

198   Vegan Crinkly Top Brownies

201   Boozy Mint Tiramisu

202   The Ultimate Chocolate Chip Cookie

204   Cherry Bakewell Blondies

206   Speculoos Millionaire Oat Bars

208   Charlie's Chocolate & Speculoos Cake

212   Neapolitan Marble Loaf

214   Triple Chocolate Muffins

216   Peach Cobbler

219   Hazelnut & Coffee Cake

221   Chocolate & Peanut Butter Self-Saucing Chocolate Cake

225   Carrot Cake Cheesecake

226   Pistachio Skillet Cookie

230   Index

236   Conversion Tables

238   Acknowledgments

WELCOME

I've often been asked: are you an appetizer person or a dessert person? Personally, I don't think we should have to pick! In fact, for me, it's quite literally impossible. Why limit yourself when you can have both sweet and savory dishes?

When it's time to make dinner and I flick through social media or cookbooks, I can almost never find everything I'm craving in one place. There might be a drool-worthy chicken bake in one book, but no desserts that take my fancy, or a pan of delicious-looking muffins in another, without a main to pair it with.

So welcome to *Sugar & Spice*, a cookbook I designed for people like me: home cooks who are short on time and don't want an overly long list of ingredients, but still want to treat themselves to dinner and dessert. People who, yes, love a slice of cake and a cup of tea—but also need a hearty pasta dish to fill them up. That's why you'll find a little bit of everything in this book: salty, cheesy Not-Birria Tacos (see page 32), a creamy, boozy tiramisu with a "healthy" portion of chocolate on top (see page 201), and oh, the fiery kick of shito, a Ghanaian chile oil sensation (see page 131)—all the good stuff.

In this book you will find all my beloved recipes, recognizable classics leveled-up with simple tips and techniques to pack in flavor, and easy-to-find hero ingredients that will refresh your dull dinner cycle. There are sweet and savory recipes that you will come back to again and again—easy weeknight wins, "fake-out" dishes that are as tasty as (and cheaper!) than the real thing, hearty recipes from my childhood, simple sweets in small batches for those late-night cravings, and desserts to please a crowd every single time. Whether you want sweet or savory, this book is full of irresistible comfort food for every craving.

Prepare for this cookbook to be the answer to the never-ending questions of "What's for dinner?" and "Is there dessert tonight?" Within these pages, you'll discover recipes that capture the essence of being in the kitchen—the warmth, laughter and pure satisfaction of creating (and eating!) something delicious.

Whether you're a seasoned chef or a kitchen newbie, fear not! *Sugar & Spice* is here to enhance your usual meal routine while keeping things beginner-friendly, exciting and fun. With easy-to-follow instructions, you'll be whipping up these dishes like a pro in no time. So go ahead, dive in and let the magic of good food bring comfort and joy to your kitchen.

Love Remi

ABOUT ME

Hi there! I'm Remi, and I'm beyond thrilled to be your new kitchen buddy on this flavorful journey. Here's to you becoming a master chef (prepare for the title to stick). I can't wait for you to share in my passion and love for comfort food and I truly hope this book inspires you to create delicious dishes every day.

I grew up in England with immigrant parents from Ghana and Nigeria, and my culinary adventure began pretty early—I am an African daughter after all. Being surrounded by the rich, hearty flavors of West African food, such as spice-filled groundnut soup, or a rich and flavorful yam and egusi stew, I quickly fell in love with the art of cooking. However, my upbringing also taught me the value of making the most out of what's available—there was no convincing my mom to go on an extravagant shopping trip for a single recipe with a laundry list of ingredients (especially ones we wouldn't regularly use).

With my mom's love for cooking, we grew up never ordering takeout, so my palate wasn't very diverse, but I remember my first encounter with takeout pizza at the age of 15. We all caught the flu, and with no one to cook, it was time to try the goodness of Domino's Pizza. As simple as it sounds, this was a pivotal moment that ignited my curiosity for diverse cuisines beyond our small hometown kitchen and to explore what else was out there.

As I started experimenting in my kitchen, I found so much joy in playing with flavors from different cultures. It didn't take long to discover my sweet tooth—a discovery that delighted me, but probably had my parents rolling their eyes. I threw myself into baking and my little sister Funmi and I spent hours watching American shows like *Cake Boss* and *Cupcake Wars*, and, of course, *The Great British Bake Off*. Inspired, we tried our hands at making cinnamon rolls, lemon cakes and anything else we could think of. Baking became "our thing." Whenever family or friends came over, it was practically expected that I'd bake something—on the condition I didn't make it too sweet, of course!

Years later, my sisters and I finally made a trip to New York—a city bursting with cultures and cuisines. I was thrilled to dive into Italian, Mexican and Korean dishes, all just a few blocks apart. Foods I had only ever seen on TV were now right in front of me, ready to be devoured. It was heaven for my taste buds and inspiration for my soul.

In 2018, at just 19, I took the plunge and launched Bakes by Remi. My sisters convinced me to start an Instagram page to share the cupcakes and cookies I was constantly baking. To my surprise, people didn't just admire my posts—they asked to buy my goodies, too. I said yes, of course, and soon I was selling brownies and cookies. I even coded my own website!

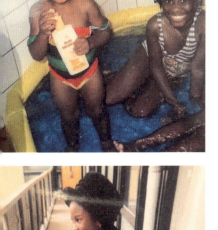

What followed were sleepless nights baking and packaging orders at 5 a.m., then heading off to my apprenticeship. It was exhausting, but the thrill of seeing my creations bring people joy kept me going. As a 19-year-old juggling a growing business and a demanding full-time job, I eventually had to make a tough call. After a few successful pop-up market stalls and countless late nights, I decided to close Bakes by Remi.

I thought that was the end of my baking journey, but it turns out it was just the beginning. I started making videos to teach people how to bake cookies and brownies, and those videos turned into something much bigger. By late 2021, I rebranded as Food by Remi, an online platform where I could share my love of food in all its forms.

Since then, I've poured my heart into creating recipes and sharing them with the world. In just three short years, that passion has helped me connect with a global audience of over 1 million enthusiastic food lovers. What started as a hobby has grown into something far bigger than I could have imagined. Now I create and develop recipes, film and edit all my videos and have the privilege to call myself a cookbook author.

COOKING 101
(basics you should know)

The one thing I love about cooking is that it's really easy to get it right, but here are some tips to make sure you get it perfect.

ONIONS

Onions are the backbone of pretty much all of my savory recipes, and like pasta, different shapes of onions can give a different taste and texture. It's important to know when to use each one and what each one looks like.

Minced
Super-fine cuts of onion are best when you need a strong burst of flavor but don't want chunks—for example, in the meatballs found on page 36.

Diced
Small, uniform cubes of onion are ideal when you want the flavor evenly distributed throughout a dish—for example, in the Beef Chow Mein on page 106.

Sliced
Long, thin strips of onion are ideal for when you want them to shine visually and hold their structure—these are used with the Chipotle Cream Enchiladas on page 46.

MY SPICE MUST-HAVES

Here's the lowdown on the spices I think every kitchen needs. Sure, it's a good-sized list, but trust me, nobody wants to live in a world where food is only seasoned with salt and pepper. And let's not even get started on dishes drowning in all-purpose seasoning. We can do better, people! Here's how:

- **Chicken bouillon powder**
  When I'm running low on salt or just want to take a dish up a notch, chicken bouillon powder is my go-to. It's packed with umami goodness that works wonders in soups, stews and rice dishes. Just don't overdo it—it's a flavor bomb, not a salt replacement for everything.

- **Kashmiri chile powder**
  Think of this as chile powder on steroids! It's vibrant, with just the right balance of heat and flavor. Perfect for curries, but honestly, it works in so many dishes when you need a little fiery kick.

- **Cinnamon & nutmeg**
  These aren't just for baking, folks! I love sneaking a pinch of cinnamon or nutmeg into tomato sauces for a subtle, warm depth. Trust me, it's a game-changer when you want to level up your pasta night.

- **Cumin seeds & cardamom**
  Earthy, warm and oh-so-aromatic. These two are a dream team for adding complexity to Indian and Middle Eastern dishes. But don't stop there—they're amazing in rice, roasted veggies and even marinades.

- **Garlic granules**
  Listen, I am unapologetically a Garlic Girl, and you'll see that throughout this book. Garlic granules are perfect for when you're too lazy to chop fresh cloves (no judgement!) but still want that garlicky punch.

- **Onion granules**
  Onions are the unsung heroes of flavor and granules are a quick and easy way to boost taste in anything from burgers to béchamel. They're a lifesaver when you're out of fresh onions—or just don't feel like chopping them.

- **Smoked paprika**
  If smoked paprika isn't in your pantry, we need to talk. It's smoky, sweet and ridiculously versatile. Whether you're making roasted potatoes, chile or marinades, this spice adds instant depth and drama.

each of the above is a powerhouse in its own right, ready to take your cooking from "meh" to "WOW." Keep them stocked and you're halfway to kitchen greatness.

GOLDEN GOODNESS

In my book, you'll see brown butter used a lot because, put simply, it's the best. Brown butter adds a depth of flavor and complexity that is unparalleled. Through the process of browning, the milk solids in the butter caramelize, resulting in a nutty aroma and a rich, toasty taste, which elevates your entire baking experience. This golden elixir infuses each bite with a warm, comforting essence, creating a perfect balance of sweetness and savory notes.

People often undercook or overcook the butter, so here are some steps to make it perfect.

1 Start by chopping your butter into even cubes. It's not just for looks—it helps it melt more evenly, so you're not stuck with a lumpy, half-melted mess. Put the cubes into a light-colored pan if you've got one. It makes it so much easier to spot when it goes from golden to brown, which is exactly what we're after (burnt butter? No, thanks!).

2 Set your heat to medium—there's no need to rush this. High heat might seem tempting, but it'll just scorch the milk solids and leave you with a burnt disaster. Let the butter melt completely and give it a stir every now and then. It's a bit like babysitting, but worth it.

3 As the butter melts, you'll notice it start to foam and bubble. That's the water evaporating—science in action! Soon enough, the foam will calm down and you'll see the milk solids at the bottom of the pan starting to brown. You'll know you're close because the sizzling will quiet down and you'll get that warm, nutty smell. It's heavenly.

4 When you hit that golden-brown color and amazing aroma, it's time to take it off the heat—don't wait! It can go from browned to burned in a flash. And here's the secret: those toasty little bits at the bottom of the pan? That's where all the flavor lives, so make sure to keep them. Stir them in, scrape them out—whatever works. They're the good stuff.

And there you go—perfect brown butter, ready to make everything it touches a little more amazing.

SECRETS TO BAKING LIKE A PRO

Baking doesn't have to be as intimidating as it seems. People love to say it's both a science and an art, but trust me—once you understand the basics, it's not nearly as daunting. Over my years of baking, I've noticed there are a few main culprits behind most baking fails, and once you know how to tackle them, you're well on your way to success. Let's make it less scary together!

1 LACK OF PATIENCE

Baking is one of those things that sometimes takes its sweet time (although you will find some speedy options if you flip to the Something Sweet chapter)! Whether it's chilling your dough or waiting for your oven to preheat, every step matters. I know it's tempting to cut corners, but trust me, rushing never pays off. Skipping the dough's rise can leave your cinnamon rolls dense and sad instead of light and fluffy. And don't even get me started on pulling a cake out of the oven too soon—raw centers and collapsing layers are heartbreakers after all your hard work. Impatience is the number one enemy of great baking. Every step in a recipe exists for a reason, and when you let the process unfold naturally, the magic happens. So, take a deep breath, grab a cup of tea and embrace the journey. Your patience will be rewarded with perfectly baked treats.

How to avoid it

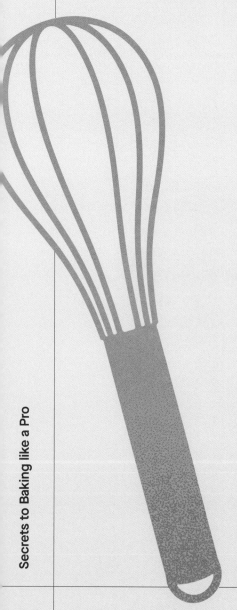

- **Bake with time on your side:** Start when you've got plenty of time. Baking under pressure is when mistakes creep in. When you're relaxed, you're more likely to follow every step perfectly and enjoy the experience.

- **Chill, relax and bake:** Baking is more than just a recipe—it's a mood! Turn on your favorite playlist or a podcast and let the steps feel like self-care. Bonus: it makes the kitchen smell even better when you're enjoying the process.

- **Prep is your best friend:** Measure and organize your ingredients before you even turn on the mixer. This not only keeps you calm but ensures your baking stays accurate. Plus, it's way less stressful when everything is at your fingertips.

- **Set a timer:** Trust the clock! Resist the urge to peek or open the oven door too often—it messes with the temperature and can throw your baking off track.

2 OVEN TEMPERATURE

Now, let's talk about ovens—those sneaky little tricksters. They can be surprisingly inconsistent, leading to underbaking, overbaking or uneven results. Even the most foolproof recipe can flop if your oven temperature is off. Why? Because baking is essentially a science experiment and heat is the catalyst for all the magical chemical reactions. Without the right heat, your bakes don't stand a chance. Think of it like growing a flower, which needs steady sunlight to thrive, right? Now imagine the sun keeps flickering on and off because you're constantly peeking into the oven to see if your "flower" is done. Or worse, your flower is trying to bloom, but the sun hasn't even finished "preheating" yet! See where I'm going with this? For your baked goods to truly shine, your oven has to stay consistent and be ready to do its job.

How to avoid it

- **Invest in an oven thermometer:** Most ovens lie. Even if you set it to 400°F (200°C), it might be 10–20 degrees off. An oven thermometer is a small, inexpensive tool that ensures you are baking at the exact temperature you need.

- **Preheat properly (and be patient):** Preheating isn't just a suggestion, it's mandatory. Most ovens take 10–15 minutes to heat up fully. Trust your thermometer rather than the preheat "beep" on your oven, which often signals too early.

- **Learn your oven's quirks:** Does one corner burn cookies while the other leaves them pale? Take note. Rotate your pans halfway through baking to avoid uneven results and adjust the rack placement for specific recipes (for example, use the middle rack for cakes and higher racks for broiling).

- **Avoid overloading the oven:** Too many pans in the oven at the same time can block airflow, leading to uneven baking. Stick to one pan at a time for delicate items like cookies or cakes, or stagger them if you're doubling a recipe.

- **Don't peek too often:** Opening the oven door too frequently can cause heat to escape, disrupting the temperature. Use the oven light and window to check on your bake instead of peeking inside every 5 minutes.

3 INCORRECT MEASUREMENTS

Unlike cooking, baking doesn't leave much room for improvisation. You can't just toss in a dash of this or a pinch of that and hope for the best. Every ingredient has a specific job to do, and even slight deviations can throw the whole recipe off balance. Too much flour? You'll end up with a dense cake or dry cookies. Cut down on sugar for a "healthier" bake? Say goodbye to that glossy, golden crust. Now, let's keep this book about good vibes, but I've got a confession: I really don't like measuring cups. They're notoriously inaccurate. One baker's "cup of flour" can weigh significantly more than another's. That's why I'll always reach for a kitchen scale—it's my secret weapon for consistency. I get that eyeballing or winging it can be tempting, but trust me: a recipe's success depends on precise ingredient ratios.

How to avoid it

- **Whip out a kitchen scale:** A kitchen scale is a baker's best friend. It's affordable, easy to find online or in stores and worth every penny. With a scale, you can weigh ingredients, ensuring accuracy and perfect results every single time.

- **Measure sticky ingredients with ease:** Sticky ingredients like honey or molasses can cling to your measuring tools. The trick? Lightly coat your measuring spoon with a bit of oil before scooping or adding the sticky stuff. It will slide right out, leaving no precious drops behind!

- **For cup lovers:** When in doubt, remember that for liquids: 1 cup = 240 ml, 1 tablespoon = 15 ml and 1 teaspoon = 5 ml. Other ingredients vary depending on the ingredient used. Also, when measuring flour, spoon it into the cup and level it off with a knife—don't scoop directly from the bag, as it packs in more than you need.

4   USING THE WRONG PAN

So, you've nailed the recipe—measured, mixed and followed every step perfectly—then you realize you don't have the right pan size. No biggie, right? Just grab one that's a little different and hope for the best. Unfortunately, it's not that simple. Take the fudgiest brownies ever (page 198, and yes, you have to try them!). The size of the pan is just as important as the ingredients. If it is too small, your batter will rise and overflow into a sticky, bubbly mess. If it's too big, you'll end up with sad, flat, dry brownies. It's not just about size either—shape and material matter too. A deeper pan changes baking times and a dark metal pan bakes differently than a glass or aluminum one. These details can make or break your bake, but don't worry—I've got some tips to help you choose (or adapt) the perfect pan every time.

How to avoid it

- **Stick to the recipe:** Recipes usually specify pan size for a reason. If it calls for an 8 in (20 cm) round cake pan, resist the urge to grab a 9 in (23 cm) one. If you don't have the right size, try adjusting the batter amount or baking time.

- **Understand volume:** If you don't have the exact pan size, check the volume of the one you have. For example, an 8 in (20 cm) round pan holds about 6 cups (1.4 liters) of batter, while a 9 in (23 cm) pan holds about 8 cups (1.9 liters). If you're scaling up or down, ensure the batter fits without exceeding two-thirds of the pan's height.

- **Adjust baking times:** If you're using a pan that's slightly different from what's called for:
  - For smaller pans, reduce the oven temperature slightly (by about 10°) and increase the baking time. Keep a close eye on the bake to prevent over-browning.
  - For larger pans, increase the oven temperature slightly and reduce the baking time because the batter will be more thinly spread and bake faster.

5   NOT STICKING TO THE RECIPE

I know it's tempting (and very on-trend) to "go with the flow," but when it comes to baking, I can't stress this enough: until you've nailed the basics, stick to the recipe. Straying too far from instructions might leave you with results that are, let's say, less than delightful. Trust me on this—I've spent hours testing every recipe in this book so that they work perfectly. Think of it like building a house. If you follow the blueprint, you'll end up with something sturdy, reliable and beautiful. Once you've mastered the foundations, then you can play around and make it your own. So take a deep breath, trust the process and follow the recipe.

GET INTO THE BOOK

Now you've got to grips with the basics, here's what you can expect in the rest of this book...

CHAPTER ONE: *CLASSICS WITH A TWIST*

We all know how to make classic staples, but it's time to make them even better. These are my takes on everyone's favorite home-cooked dishes, designed to be as decadent and delicious as they are simple and satisfying.

CHAPTER TWO: *FRIDAY NIGHT CRAVINGS*

As much as I love the question, "What are we ordering tonight?" sometimes there's rice at home... Plus there's nothing worse than ordering takeout when you know you can make it just as tasty at home—because you can!—and save money at the same time. This chapter goes through all the fan favorites with tips and tricks to keep the food juicy, crispy and delicious.

CHAPTER THREE: *CHILDHOOD*

We're taking it all the way back to the 1990s with this chapter. This is the food I grew up eating all the time: hearty, rich African food, made with fresh staple ingredients. We all know the saying "Mama knows best," so these have all been double-checked by my mom to ensure you have everything you need to recreate an African kitchen in your home.

CHAPTER FOUR: *A LITTLE SOMETHING SWEET*

If you are a bit like me, you're always craving a little sweet treat after dinner. This chapter has the easy, quick dessert recipes you can whip up without having to labor for hours. There are single-serve ideas and something for kids, too. Based on my popular "Something Sweet" series online, I know you'll love these.

CHAPTER FIVE: *DESSERTS TO IMPRESS*

Everyone deserves something special at the end of the day (or beginning, I'm not judging!). These desserts are showstoppers, not only for dinner parties and guests, but also for when you want a sweet bite to pick you up. From cookies to cakes to doughnuts, there's something for everyone.

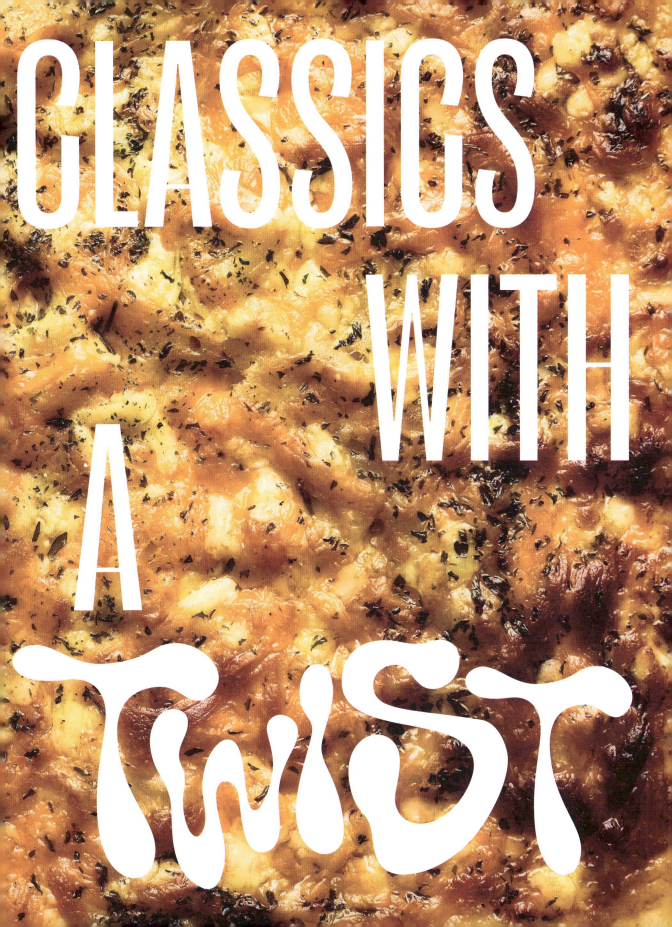

CLASSICS WITH A TWIST

Italian Sausage *Lasagna*

My sisters and I each have our own unique way of making lasagna. Funmi insists on starting with a classic mirepoix, while Queeny skips boiling the pasta sheets and goes for extra layers. My secret weapon? Italian sausage. Unfortunately, I wasn't born in the US where you can find it easily in stores, so I make my own version at home. When it's added to this lasagna, it takes the dish to a whole new level—ten times better, if you ask me!

Serves 8

About 1 lb (450 g) fresh
    lasagna sheets
7 oz (200 g) Cheddar, grated
3½ oz (100 g) Red Leicester (or
    Wisconsin Cheddar), grated
4½ oz (125 g) mozzarella, sliced

For the Italian sausage mix
9 oz (250 g) pork sausage meat
2 tsp fennel seeds
1 tsp white pepper
2 tsp chile flakes
1 tsp garlic granules
1 tsp onion granules

For the meat sauce
2 tbsp olive oil
6 garlic cloves, minced
1 lb 2 oz (500 g) 20% fat
    ground beef
1 red onion, diced
28 oz (800 g) can chopped
    tomatoes
Scant ½ cup (100 ml) water
½ tsp nutmeg
1 tsp paprika
1 tbsp Italian seasoning
1 oz (30 g) fresh basil
1 sprig of rosemary
Parmesan rind (optional,
    but it's really worth it)

For the béchamel sauce
7 tbsp (100 g) butter
⅔ cup (75 g) all-purpose flour
3¾–4¼ cups (900 ml–
    1 liter) milk
1 tsp onion granules
1 tsp garlic granules
Salt and pepper

1   In a bowl, combine all the ingredients for the Italian sausage mix.

2   To make the meat sauce, heat the oil in a large pot over medium heat, add the garlic and sauté for about 1 minute until fragrant. Add the beef and Italian sausage mix and cook until the meat is browned all over, breaking it apart with a wooden spoon as it cooks. Add the onion, cover with a lid and cook for 3–5 minutes until softened. Remove the lid and cook for another 5 minutes until most of the liquid has evaporated.

3   Add the chopped tomatoes and water. Increase the heat to high and cook for about 5 minutes until the sauce thickens. Reduce the heat to low, add the remaining ingredients and stir to combine, then re-cover and cook gently for 30 minutes, stirring occasionally. Remove the Parmesan rind, if using.

4   Meanwhile, make the béchamel. Melt the butter in a sauté pan over medium heat, add the flour and cook for about 2 minutes, whisking continuously to form a paste. Gradually add the milk (it's important to not add this all at once or the sauce will be lumpy), whisking constantly, until the sauce is smooth and has reached your desired thickness (you may not need all the milk; see Tip). Add the onion granules, garlic granules and half of the Cheddar and stir until the cheese is fully melted and the sauce is smooth and creamy. Season with salt and pepper to taste. Set aside.

5   Preheat your oven to 400°F (200°C).

Continued overleaf

TIP

When making the béchamel sauce, you want it to be thinner than the final consistency needed, since it will continue to thicken as it bakes.

6 To assemble your lasagna, spread a thin layer of the meat sauce over the bottom of a 9 × 13 in (23 × 33 cm) baking dish. Place a layer of lasagna sheets on top of the sauce. Spread a layer of the meat sauce over the pasta, followed by a layer of béchamel sauce. Repeat the layering until you have used up the meat sauce but have some pasta sheets and béchamel remaining.

7 For the final layer, cut the remaining lasagna sheets into squares and roughly place them on top of each other (this creates a larger surface area, which makes them crunchy. Alternatively, just add the pasta sheets as before then finish with a final layer of béchamel sauce.

8 Sprinkle over the remaining Cheddar, the Red Leicester and mozzarella and bake for 25–30 minutes until the top is golden and bubbling. Let the lasagna rest for 10 minutes before slicing and serving.

TIP

If you don't eat pork, omit the sausage meat and use 9 oz (250 g) extra ground beef.

Curried Mutton *Pot Pie*

Where I grew up, there used to be a fish and chip shop that always sold Pukka Pie's All-Steak Pie. The first time I tried this meaty pot pie, I was disappointed. I loved the flaky layers, but the filling itself was quite bland. So this is a combination of an amazing meat sauce with easy ready-made puff pastry. It's a perfect fusion of flavors and ideal for a cold winter day—the veggies absorb the rich, spiced sauce and add hearty texture to the pie. For those who like a fiery kick and add the Scotch bonnet to the mix—be cautious, it packs serious heat!

Now you may be pretty full after this bad boy, but there is always room for dessert, and this pairs perfectly with the light, fresh Single-Serve Strawberry Crisp on page 144.

Makes 4 hearty portions

3 lb 5 oz (600 g) boneless mutton, diced
1 tsp black pepper
2 tbsp hot curry powder
1 tsp ground turmeric
1 tsp allspice
3 tbsp vegetable/sunflower oil
1 red onion, diced
4 garlic cloves, minced
Thumb-sized piece of ginger, minced
2 sprigs of thyme
2 cups (500 ml) water
2 potatoes (about 9 oz/250 g), peeled and diced
1 small carrot, sliced
1 Scotch bonnet chile, sliced (optional)
1 sheet of all-butter puff pastry
Salt, to taste

For the egg wash
1 large egg
1 tsp curry powder

TIP

When you've cooked your curried mutton, you can either put it in the large family-sized dish as here or in individual pie dishes, or save some in an airtight container in the fridge and serve it with rice the next day.

1 First up, put the mutton into a bowl and season with the pepper, hot curry powder, turmeric, allspice and salt, making sure the meat is well coated. I recommend wearing food-safe gloves for this, as the spices can easily stain your hands.

2 Heat the oil in a large pot over medium–high heat. When the oil is hot, add the mutton and cook until browned on all sides (this locks in those rich flavors). Next, add the onion, garlic, ginger and thyme and cook, stirring, for about 2 minutes until the mixture becomes fragrant. Pour in the water, or just enough to cover the mutton, and bring to a gentle boil, then reduce the heat to low, cover with a lid and cook gently for about 2 hours until the mutton is tender and has soaked up all the flavors. Keep an eye on it, adding more water if needed. Remember, if you add water, taste the broth and adjust the seasoning as needed.

3 When the mutton is tender, toss in the potatoes, carrot and chile, if using, and cook until the veggies are soft, which should take about 20–30 minutes.

4 As the filling finishes cooking, preheat your oven to 425°F (220°C) and take the puff pastry out of the fridge to allow it to come to room temperature (this makes it easier to work with).

5 Transfer the curried mutton mixture to an 8 in (20 cm) pie dish, making sure it is evenly spread. Unroll the pastry sheet and lay it over the top of the dish, crimp the edges, then trim off any excess. Press the pastry gently against the rim to seal in all that goodness and cut a few small slits in the top to allow the steam to escape.

6 In a small bowl, whisk together the egg wash ingredients, then brush over the top of the pastry to give the pie a beautiful golden color and a hint of extra flavor. Bake for 20–25 minutes or until the pastry is golden and puffed up.

Gochujang *Chicken Kyiv*

I can't quite remember the first time I had chicken Kyiv, but wow, do I love it. The crispy chicken coating, the buttery garlic filling—every bite is an explosion of flavors. Since this chapter is all about elevating classics, I'm adding a pantry favorite: gochujang. It brings a fantastic kick that takes the traditional Kyiv to a whole new level.

These would work great the next day heated up in a chicken Caesar-like salad.

Serves 4

4 skinless, boneless chicken breasts
Heaped ¾ cup (100 g) all-purpose flour
2 eggs
2 cups (100 g) panko breadcrumbs
2 tbsp sesame seeds
2 tbsp black sesame seeds
2 tsp salt
1 tsp black pepper
Vegetable/sunflower oil, for frying

For the gochujang garlic butter
10 tbsp (150 g) salted butter, softened
3 tbsp chopped fresh parsley
2 tbsp gochujang paste
4 garlic cloves, minced
2 tsp salt

1 First, make the gochujang garlic butter. Combine all the ingredients in a mixing bowl, mixing thoroughly until well combined. Spoon the mixture onto plastic wrap or parchment paper, forming it into a rectangular shape. Wrap tightly and place in the freezer for at least 30 minutes until firm (If it's too soft, you won't be able to stuff it into the chicken).

2 Meanwhile, prepare the chicken. Using a sharp knife, slice through each chicken breast from top to bottom horizontally, being careful not to cut all the way through, to form a cavity big enough for the butter but not so large that it seeps out when cooking.

3 When the butter is firm, cut it into 4 equal pieces, then put a piece into each pocket in the chicken.

4 Now set up a breading station with 3 shallow dishes. Put the flour into the first dish, beat the eggs with a pinch of salt in the second dish and finally, mix the panko breadcrumbs, sesame seeds (both black and white), salt and pepper in the third dish.

5 To make things easier, have one wet hand and one dry hand. Using your wet hand, carefully dip each chicken breast into the egg mixture, then dredge it in the flour. Dip it again into the beaten eggs, ensuring it is fully coated. Finally, place it in the breadcrumb mixture and, using your dry hand, press it into the mixture, making sure the chicken is evenly coated and the seal is well covered to ensure the butter won't seep out.

6 Preheat your oven to 400°F (200°C).

7 Heat a generous amount of oil in a large ovenproof skillet over medium heat. When hot, add the chicken and cook for 3–4 minutes on each side until golden brown. Transfer to the oven and bake for 20–25 minutes until cooked through. Allow to rest for a few minutes before serving.

Not-Birria *Tacos*

Like many people in the UK I was first introduced to birria tacos on TikTok—they looked delicious and I loved trying them at food markets. Ancho and guajillo chilies are not easily accessible where I live (use them if you can get them!)—so these are not birria tacos but pretty good regardless!

If you have any leftover meat and sauce, they work perfectly with some gyros and tzatziki!

Serves 6

2 red peppers, halved and deseeded
2 pointed peppers, halved and deseeded
1 large onion, roughly chopped
2 beefsteak tomatoes, roughly chopped
1 garlic bulb, cloves peeled
2 cups (500 ml) chicken stock
3 lb 5 oz (1.5 kg) pork shoulder joint, fat removed and cut into chunks
1 tbsp dried thyme
1 tbsp smoked paprika
1 tsp black pepper
2 bay leaves
2 tsp salt
Vegetable/sunflower oil, for frying

For the tacos
18 mini tortillas
3½ oz (100 g) mozzarella, grated
½ onion, diced

1 Heat a little oil in a large pot over medium heat, add all the peppers, skin-side down, and cook until charred. To speed up the process, you can put something heavy on top of the vegetables like a grill press. Transfer the peppers to a blender, add the onion, tomatoes, garlic and stock and blend until smooth.

2 Add some more oil to the same pot. Working in batches to avoid overcrowding, add the pork and cook for 5–7 minutes until browned on all sides (this helps build flavor in the broth). Pour in the onion and tomato mixture, then add the thyme, smoked paprika, pepper, bay leaves and salt and stir to combine and coat the meat. Bring to a boil, then reduce the heat to low, cover with a lid and cook gently for 2–3 hours until the pork is tender and can be easily shredded.

3 Carefully remove the pork from the pot and shred using 2 forks, then return the meat to the broth and stir well until it is coated in the sauce. Cook gently over low heat for 10–15 minutes to allow the flavors to meld. Remove from the heat.

4 Heat a dry skillet over medium heat. Warm a mini tortilla in the hot pan for about 30 seconds on each side until pliable and slightly charred, then lightly dip into the pork broth to coat it. Spoon some of the shredded pork onto one half of the tortilla and sprinkle with some mozzarella, then fold in half like a taco. Repeat with the remaining tortillas, shredded pork and mozzarella.

5 Working in batches, cook the folded tacos in the same skillet for 2–3 minutes on each side until crispy and the cheese has melted. Serve with the onion sprinkled on top and a small bowl of the pork broth on the side for dipping.

TIP

It is best to cook the pork in batches to ensure the meat sears, rather than steams in an overcrowded pan.

Vodka & 'Nduja *Rigatoni*

Who remembers the watery tomato pasta pots school used to sell? Well now we are grown up, these are the vodka pasta adult version. Don't worry if you don't like the taste of vodka, it just adds a nice kick.

Pasta is the key to a perfect meal, baby! Let's finish it off with the Single-Serve Cinnamon Roll on page 141.

Makes 2 hearty portions

7 oz (200 g) dried rigatoni
2 tbsp olive oil
2 garlic cloves, minced
2 tsp chile flakes
3½ tbsp tomato paste
3½ tbsp 'nduja paste
Scant ½ cup (100 ml) vodka
⅔ cup (150 ml) heavy cream
1¾ oz (50 g) Parmesan, grated
1 tsp black pepper
Salt

1   Start by cooking the rigatoni in a large pot of salted boiling water according to the package instructions until al dente. Drain, reserving a mug full of the pasta water to loosen up the sauce later. Set aside the pasta.

2   Meanwhile, heat the oil in a large sauté pan over medium heat, add the garlic and chile flakes and sauté for about a minute until fragrant but not browned. Stir in the tomato paste and 'nduja paste and cook for another few minutes until the tomato paste is slightly caramelized (this helps to intensify the flavor of the sauce). Reduce the heat and carefully pour in the vodka, stirring well to deglaze the pan. Cook gently for a couple of minutes until the alcohol evaporates and the sauce thickens slightly.

3   Reduce the heat to low, then stir in the cream until you have a smooth, rich sauce. Cook gently for a few minutes to thicken the sauce and allow the flavor to develop. Add the Parmesan, stirring until melted. Season with the pepper, and salt to taste, but go easy with it as both the 'nduja and cheese are quite salty.

4   Toss the cooked rigatoni into the sauce, stirring until the pasta is evenly coated. If the sauce feels too thick, add a splash of the reserved pasta water to loosen it up, then serve.

TIP

'Nduja is a spicy, spreadable pork sausage from the Calabria region of Italy. Look for it in Italian delis and international grocery stores.

Spaghetti & Lamb *Harissa Meatballs*

Italians, look away! I'm sorry (but not really) because this is not your traditional spaghetti and meatballs. Dare I say … it's even better! Swapping the beef for lamb makes these meatballs super juicy, and paired with harissa and mint, they will leave your mouth salivating. This dish can be made in under an hour, making it perfect for a midweek meal, too.

After you slop this up with garlic bread, why not sweeten the deal with my air fryer doughnuts (see page 168)?

Makes 4 hearty portions

For the meatballs
1 lb 2 oz (500 g) ground lamb
½ onion, finely diced or grated
Handful of fresh mint, chopped
3½ oz (100 g) harissa paste
    (get a good-quality one; you
    can taste the difference!)
1 tsp salt

For the tomato sauce
2 tbsp oil
½ onion, diced
4 large garlic cloves, minced
14 oz (400 g) can chopped
    tomatoes
1¼ cups (300 ml) water
2 tsp salt
1 tsp black pepper

To serve
Chopped fresh parsley
Cooked spaghetti
Garlic bread

1 Preheat your oven to 425°F (220°C) and line a baking sheet with parchment paper.

2 Combine all the ingredients for the meatballs in a large bowl, then mix until they emulsify—trust me, it's nothing scary: this occurs when the mixture becomes smooth, sticky and uniformly combined and holds together well. Form the mixture into roughly 10–12 meatballs, making them slightly larger than you want as they will shrink when baked. Transfer to the prepared pan and bake for 15 minutes (don't worry if they're not fully cooked, as we'll be adding them to the sauce later).

3 Meanwhile, make the tomato sauce. Heat the oil in a large pot over medium heat, add the onion and sauté until translucent, then add the garlic and cook until fragrant. Add the chopped tomatoes, then fill the can with the water and pour into the pan. Stir to combine and season with the salt and pepper. Reduce the heat to low and cook gently, uncovered.

4 Remove the meatballs from the oven and carefully transfer them to the tomato sauce. Add any juices and fat from the baking sheet to the sauce (these add extra flavor and richness so please don't throw them away). Cook gently for another 20 minutes to allow the flavors to meld and until the meatballs are cooked through.

5 Garnish with parsley and serve with spaghetti and my favorite, garlic bread.

TIPS

In this recipe, we want the onion pieces to be tiny—if you're not confident with your chopping skills, grate the onion. If you have leftover meatballs, when cooled, transfer them to an airtight container and refrigerate for up to 3 days. They work great as a meatball sub. Top with some mozzarella and that's lunch taken care of!

Roast Chicken with Rosemary Salt Potatoes & *Salsa Verde*

A classic roast dinner needs a British-themed dessert and my Earl Grey Tres Leches Cake on page 188 is the perfect pairing.

While many people have fond memories of gathering around the table on a Sunday to have a classic British roast dinner, that was never really my family's vibe. We had jollof rice (see page 114), chicken and plantain. However, now I've started making it more, this is how I always cook roast chicken for my fiancé.

Rather than cook it whole, I spatchcock the chicken, which helps it cook evenly and reduces the cooking time. Spreading it with herb butter and lemon adds flavor and keeps the chicken moist. Adding baking soda when boiling the potatoes helps to break down their surface and give them a beautifully crispy finish.

For a final twist, I serve this classic with a fragrant salsa verde, which adds a bright, fresh contrast to the richness of the roast chicken.

Serves 4

3–4 lb (1.4–1.8 kg) whole chicken
14 tbsp (200 g) salted butter, softened
4 garlic cloves, minced
2 tsp salt
1 tsp black pepper
1 tsp fresh thyme, minced
2 tsp fresh parsley, minced
2 lemons, sliced

For the rosemary salt potatoes
1 tbsp baking soda
2 lb 10 oz (1.2 kg) roasting potatoes (like Yukon gold), washed and cut into quarters or halves, depending on size
Scant ½ cup (100 ml) vegetable oil
6 sprigs of rosemary
1 tbsp salt, or to taste

For the salsa verde
4 garlic cloves, crushed
2 tsp capers
1¾ oz (50 g) anchovy fillets
3½ tbsp olive oil
3–4 tbsp chopped parsley
½ cup (15 g) fresh mint, chopped
½ cup (15 g) fresh rosemary, chopped

1   Preheat your oven to 425°F (220°C) and line a roasting pan with parchment paper.

2   To spatchcock the chicken, place it breast-side down on a chopping board. Cut along both sides of the backbone using sharp kitchen scissors, removing it entirely. Turn the chicken over and press down firmly on the breastbone to flatten the bird, then place on the prepared roasting pan.

3   In a bowl, mix together the butter, garlic, salt, pepper, thyme and parsley. Gently pull the skin away from the chicken breast and thighs, being careful not to tear it. Rub some of the herb butter under the skin. Rub the remaining butter all over the outside of the chicken, not forgetting the side touching the paper. Tuck at least 1 lemon slice under the skin of each breast and thigh, then place the remaining slices underneath the chicken.

4   Cover in foil and roast the chicken for 45–60 minutes, depending on its size, removing the foil midway through, until the skin is golden brown and crispy and the internal temperature of the thickest part of the breast reaches 170°F (75°C) or the juices run clear.

5   Meanwhile, cook the potatoes. Line a large baking pan with parchment paper. Bring a large pot of water to a boil, add the baking soda and potatoes and cook for 8–10 minutes until just tender but not fully cooked. Drain, then let steam dry for a few minutes. Transfer to the lined baking pan and pour over the oil, then coat the potatoes thoroughly in the oil. Spread out in a single layer, skin-side up.

6   Pick the leaves from 4 sprigs of the rosemary, add the salt, then crush using a mortar and pestle to make a fragrant rosemary salt. Sprinkle generously over the potatoes and position the remaining rosemary sprigs between the potatoes. Roast the potatoes with the chicken for 30–35 minutes until golden and crispy.

7   While the chicken and potatoes are roasting, combine all the salsa verde ingredients in a food processor and process until still slightly chunky.

8   When the chicken is cooked, remove from the oven and let it rest for about 10 minutes to let the juices redistribute throughout the meat. Carve the chicken and drizzle over the salsa verde. Serve with the crispy rosemary salt potatoes.

TIP

Capers and anchovies can be very salty, so my salsa verde is without salt. If you do choose to season it, taste the salsa before adding salt.

Braised Beef Short Ribs *with Stilton Mash*

As soon as the weather starts to cool, I'm all in for this recipe. Don't worry if you can't get your hands on short ribs. Any slow-cooking cut of beef works wonderfully, even a whole beef pot roast. If you're using beef chuck, just cut it into tennis ball-sized chunks for that perfect braise.

Serves 4–5

5–6 beef short ribs or braising beef (6½ lb/3 kg in total)
2 tsp salt
2 tsp black pepper
4 tbsp olive oil
1 large onion, diced
5 celery stalks, chopped
2 carrots, chopped
2 cups (500 ml) dry red wine
4¼ cups (1 liter) beef stock
10 sprigs of rosemary
1 garlic bulb, cloves peeled
2 bay leaves
1 tsp cornstarch mixed with 1½ tsp water
Salt and pepper

For the Stilton mash
1 lb 12 oz (800 g) potatoes (like Yukon gold), peeled and cut into even-sized chunks
Scant ½ cup (100 ml) 2% milk
1 tbsp salted butter
1¾ oz (50 g) Stilton (or Roquefort, Gorgonzola, or any blue cheese), plus extra if you really like the flavor

1 Preheat your oven to 425°F (220°C).

2 Season the beef generously with the salt and pepper. Heat the oil over medium–high heat in a large Dutch oven. Working in batches to avoid overcrowding the pot (if it is too full, the beef will steam not fry), sear the short ribs on all sides until very dark and caramelized (this is crucial for building flavor). Once browned, remove and set aside.

3 Add the onion, celery and carrots to the pot and cook for about 5 minutes, or until the vegetables begin to soften. Pour in the wine and stock and deglaze the pot, using a spoon to scrape any browned bits from the bottom. Add the rosemary, garlic and bay leaves and stir.

4 Cover with a lid or foil to lock in the flavor, then transfer to the oven for about 4 hours, checking occasionally that the liquid is cooking gently and adding more stock if needed, until the meat is tender and pulls away from the bone.

5 Towards the end of the ribs' braising time, make the Stilton mash. Put the potatoes into a large pot, cover with cold water and add some salt. Bring to a boil, then reduce the heat to low and cook for 15–20 minutes until you can poke a fork through with no resistance. Heat the milk and butter in a small saucepan over low heat until the butter has melted and the mixture is warm but not boiling (this helps the potatoes absorb the liquid).

6 Drain the potatoes, then return them to the pot. Give them a good mash using a potato masher or ricer—whichever you prefer—until smooth. Slowly pour in the warm milk and butter mixture, stirring as you go until your mash is nice and creamy. Season with salt and pepper to taste. Crumble in the Stilton and stir until it is fully melted and incorporated. Taste and add more Stilton if you like a bolder flavor.

7 Remove the pot from the oven and transfer the ribs to a side plate. Pass the sauce through a sieve into a clean pan. Add the cornstarch to the sauce, then whisk until thickened. Serve the ribs with the Stilton mash and pour the sauce on top.

TIP

Worried about the wine? Don't be! Most of the alcohol cooks out, but if you'd rather skip it, simply swap the wine for an equal amount of beef stock. You'll still get that rich, hearty flavor.

Spicy Burnt Sausage *Pasta*

Who has never burned a sausage? Not me. This dish was created on a lazy Sunday afternoon when I wanted some creamy, carby goodness but had burned my sausages. I carried on and realized it tasted even better. This is a large single-serve portion because sometimes you just need a bowl of pasta for yourself.

A single-serve pasta needs a single-serve dessert, and fresh Single-Serve Strawberry Crisp (page 144) will cut through the creamy goodness in the pasta.

Serves 1

2½ oz (75 g) of your favorite pasta (I recommend rigatoni or paccheri, but I won't judge you for using penne)
1 tsp vegetable/sunflower oil
6 oz (170 g) sweet Italian or Irish-style sausages, skins removed
1 tsp fennel seeds
2 tsp chile flakes
3½ tbsp heavy cream
1 tsp fresh parsley
1¾ oz (50 g) Parmesan, grated, plus extra to serve
Salt

1 Start by cooking the pasta in a pot of salted boiling water according to the package instructions until al dente.

2 Meanwhile, heat your oil in a large skillet or frying pan over medium heat. When hot, add the sausage meat and sear for 3–5 minutes, without breaking down the sausages or moving them around, until nicely browned, then break apart the meat with a spoon and cook until cooked through. Stir in the fennel seeds and chile flakes and cook until fragrant, then reduce the heat to low and pour in the cream.

3 Drain the pasta, reserving a ladle's worth of the pasta water, then add the pasta and pasta water to the sausage mixture and toss well, making sure the pasta is evenly coated. Sprinkle over the parsley and Parmesan and toss once more.

4 Serve immediately with more Parmesan and enjoy!

Chipotle Cream *Enchiladas*

I tried these enchiladas on a solo trip to Barcelona after a groggy night flight and they blew my mind—a completely new flavor palette I wasn't used to. Since then, I have searched the internet to learn how to make traditional enchiladas and have been shocked by how different they are from the ones I've tried in England. This is my favorite way of making them now, and I'm sure these will be your new favorite, too. If you can, splurge on a good chipotle paste; all the flavors come from it.

Makes 12 enchiladas

3 lb 5 oz (600 g) skinless, boneless chicken breasts
2 tsp paprika
2 tsp salt
2 tsp black pepper
Generous ¾ cup (200 ml) vegetable oil
12 mini white tortillas
7 oz (200 g) ball of mozzarella, shredded

For the chipotle cream sauce
2 beefsteak tomatoes, halved
½ onion
1 tsp chicken bouillon powder
3 garlic cloves
Scant ½ cup (100 ml) heavy cream
¼ cup (50 g) cream cheese
3½ oz (100 g) chipotle paste (I use Gran Luchito Chipotle Chile Paste)
Salt, to taste

To serve (optional)
Chopped fresh parsley
Sliced onions

TIP

Make sure not to fry the tortillas for too long or they will be hard to wrap later on.

1 Start with the sauce. Put the tomatoes, onion and bouillon powder into a pot and add enough water to cover, then cover with a lid and cook over a low heat for about 15 minutes until the tomatoes and onion are soft. Reserving the stock, transfer the tomatoes and onion to a blender, along with the garlic, cream, cream cheese and chipotle paste and blend until smooth and creamy. If the sauce feels too thick, loosen it with some of the reserved stock. Taste and adjust the seasoning with a little salt if needed, then set aside.

2 Put the chicken breasts into a pot and cover with the remaining reserved stock (top up with more water if it isn't covered). Bring to a boil and cook for about 25 minutes, or until cooked through and tender, then remove from the stock. Shred the chicken with 2 forks and transfer to a bowl. Sprinkle over the paprika, salt and pepper, then toss together, making sure the chicken is well coated. Set aside.

3 Preheat your oven to 400°F (200°C).

4 Heat some of the oil in a frying pan over medium heat. When the oil is hot, add a tortilla and fry for about 30 seconds on each side until golden and flexible (this prevents them from becoming soggy later). Remove from the pan and drain on paper towels to remove the excess oil. Repeat with the remaining oil and tortillas.

5 Now, take each fried tortilla and spoon some of the seasoned chicken into the center. Roll up each one tightly and set aside while you make the next. Pour about a third of the chipotle cream sauce into the bottom of a baking dish and spread out into an even layer. Place the rolled tortillas seam-side down in the dish so they fit snugly, then pour over the remaining sauce, ensuring every tortilla is covered.

6 Sprinkle the mozzarella over the enchiladas and bake for 10–15 minutes until the cheese is melted, golden and deliciously bubbly. Feel free to serve garnished with parsley and onions for a touch of freshness.

Brown Stew *Chicken*

One of the first meals I cooked for my Jamaican fiancé was brown stew chicken and he absolutely loved it! Since then, I've perfected the recipe, and it's become a true crowd-pleaser every time I make it.

Makes 4 hearty portions

3 lb 5 oz (1.5 kg) chicken drumsticks or bone-in thighs, skin removed (see Tip)
1 onion, diced
1 red pepper, diced
1 yellow pepper, diced
4 scallions, diced
1 tbsp vegetable/sunflower oil
2 tbsp brown sugar
1 Scotch bonnet chile, diced
bunch of thyme
2 bay leaves

For the seasoning mix
Thumb-sized piece of ginger, diced
2 tbsp Jamaican browning sauce
1 tsp curry powder
1 tsp allspice
1 tsp salt
1 tsp black pepper

1 Put your chicken and veggies into a large bowl, add all the seasoning mix ingredients and mix well, making sure all the chicken pieces are well coated. Cover and let the mixture marinate for at least 1 hour, or overnight in the fridge for a deeper flavor.

2 When you're ready to cook, heat a large pot or deep pan over medium–high heat, add the oil and sugar and caramelize until the mixture turns dark brown but not burnt. Working in small batches, add the marinated chicken pieces and turn to coat them in the caramelized sugar. Cook until browned on all sides (this gives the chicken a rich color and deep flavor). Add the marinated vegetables and cook for another few minutes, stirring everything together.

3 Pour in enough water to cover the chicken and add your chile, thyme and bay leaves. Bring to a boil, then reduce the heat to low and cook gently for 45–60 minutes until the chicken is tender and cooked through, and the sauce has thickened.

4 Before serving, taste the stew and adjust the seasoning with more salt or pepper if needed.

TIP

I recommend taking the skin off the chicken before making this, since it gets soggy when boiled.

Macaroni *Béchamel*

TikTok has taught me a lot during my culinary journey, and I will always be grateful that it led me to macaroni béchamel. This is a popular dish in Egypt, coined Egyptian mac and cheese. It has a rich tomato and beef sauce topped with pasta encased in béchamel sauce, and it's all topped with cheese. Some compare it to a Greek pastitsio, but this is seasoned way better!

This is perfect for a dinner party, as the sauce can be made the day before. Along with my Boozy Mint Tiramisu on page 201, you're in for a winner!

Serves 6–8 hearty portions

1 lb 2 oz (500 g) dried penne
5 oz (150 g) Cheddar, grated
Salt

For the meat sauce
1 tbsp olive oil
1 onion, chopped
3 garlic cloves, minced
1 lb 2 oz (500 g) 20% fat
    ground beef
1 tsp ground cinnamon
1 tsp freshly grated nutmeg
    (ground nutmeg will work
    if you can't find fresh)
1 tsp salt
1 tsp black pepper
14 oz (400 g) can chopped
    tomatoes
2 tbsp tomato paste

For the béchamel sauce
7 tbsp (100 g) butter
6 tbsp (50 g) all-purpose flour
3¾–6⅓ cups (900 ml–
    1.5 liters) milk
1 tsp nutmeg
1 tsp salt
1 tsp black pepper

1 Start with the meat sauce. Heat the oil in a large saucepan or pot over medium heat, add the onion and sauté until translucent, then add your garlic and cook until fragrant. Add the beef and cook until browned, breaking it apart with a spoon as it cooks. Stir in the cinnamon, nutmeg, salt and pepper, then add the chopped tomatoes and tomato paste, reduce the heat to low and cook gently for 20–30 minutes until the sauce thickens. Adjust the seasoning to taste, then remove from the heat and leave to cool.

2 Meanwhile, cook the penne in a large pot of salted boiling water according to the package instructions until al dente, then drain and set aside.

3 To make the béchamel sauce, melt the butter in a saucepan over medium heat, then add the flour a tablespoon at a time, stirring continuously to create a paste. Cook for a minute or two, but do not let it brown. Gradually add about 1¼ cups (300 ml) of the milk at a time, whisking constantly, until the sauce is smooth and has reached your desired thickness (you may not need all the milk; see Tip). Lastly, stir in the nutmeg, salt and pepper. Set aside.

4 Preheat your oven to 400°F (200°C).

5 To assemble, pour 80% of the béchamel sauce into a bowl, add the cooked penne and combine. Put half of the penne mixture into a large baking dish, then add the meat sauce. Top with the remaining penne mixture and pour over the remaining béchamel.

6 Sprinkle with the cheese and bake for 25–30 minutes until golden brown and heated through. Allow to cool for a few minutes before serving.

TIP

When making the béchamel sauce, you want it to be thinner than the final consistency needed, as it will continue to thicken as it bakes.

Three-Cheese *Mac & Cheese*

Mac and cheese is a comfort food beloved by all, and I like to think this is the ultimate, perfect version. My sisters always delightfully rejoice when they see I'm making this for dinner. Although it's traditionally a side dish, I believe this deserves the spotlight as the main attraction on your plate. Cheesy, creamy carbs ... is there anything better?

Makes 8 hearty portions

1 lb (450 g) dried macaroni
6 oz (175 g) Cheddar, grated
5 oz (150 g) Red Leicester (or Wisconsin Cheddar), grated
4½ oz (125 g) low-moisture mozzarella, grated
Salt

For the cheese sauce
7 tbsp (100 g) butter
⅔ cup (75 g) all-purpose flour
1 tbsp paprika
1 tbsp onion granules
1 tbsp garlic granules
1 tbsp Dijon mustard
4¼ cups (1 liter) milk
1 tbsp dried parsley

1 Preheat your oven to 400°F (200°C).

2 Cook the macaroni in a large pot of salted boiling water according to the package instructions until al dente. Drain and set aside.

3 Next, make the cheese sauce. Melt the butter in a large sauté pan over medium heat, then add the flour a tablespoon at a time, stirring continuously until it forms a paste. Add the paprika, onion granules, garlic granules and mustard and stir well to combine. Gradually add about 1 cup (250 ml) of the milk at a time, whisking constantly, until the sauce is smooth and has thickened (this gradual addition helps prevent lumps). Be patient; it's worth it! Add half of the Cheddar and Red Leicester and stir until completely melted and the sauce is velvety.

4 Gently fold the cooked macaroni into the cheese sauce, ensuring every piece is coated. Transfer the mixture to a baking dish and sprinkle over the remaining Cheddar, Red Leicester and mozzarella, then the parsley.

5 Bake for 15–20 minutes, then transfer your mac & cheese to the broiler and cook for 10 minutes until the cheesy topping is crunchy.

TIP

If there's any left, store your mac and cheese in an airtight container in the fridge for up to 3 days and reheat with a small amount of milk to keep things creamy.

Beef *Patties*

Beef patties are a universal love language if you ask me. Rich spiced ground beef encased in a flaky spiced pastry ... They're spectacular. A huge shoutout to Jamaica for this one.

patties are made to be shared (unfortunately) but it does give you an excuse to make a dessert to be shared—what better than Brown Butter Banana Bread (see page 196)?

Makes 6–8 patties

For the dough
10 tbsp (150 g) cold butter, cubed
3¾ cups (450 g) all-purpose flour
2 tbsp curry powder
1 tbsp ground turmeric
1 tbsp salt
Scant ½ cup (100 ml) ice-cold water
1¾ tbsp lard, frozen
Scant ½ cup (100 ml) cold milk
1 egg, beaten

For the filling
Vegetable/sunflower oil, for frying
1 onion, chopped
1 carrot, grated
4 garlic cloves, minced
1 lb 2 oz (500 g) ground beef
1 tbsp smoked paprika
1 tsp black pepper
2 tsp curry powder
⅓ cup (25 g) fresh white breadcrumbs
Scant ½ cup (100 ml) water
1 tsp soy sauce
1 tbsp Jamaican browning sauce
Salt

1 Start with the dough. Place the cold butter in the freezer for 5 minutes until it is very cold, but not frozen solid like the lard.

2 In a large mixing bowl, combine the flour, spices and salt.

3 Using a pastry cutter or a fork, or cold hands, cut the cold butter into the flour mixture until you see small pea-sized chunks (it's essential to see visible pieces—this is what creates those beautiful, flaky layers). Gradually add the ice-cold water and cold milk a little at a time, stirring with a wooden spoon until the dough just comes together. Form into a rough ball, wrap in plastic wrap and refrigerate for 30 minutes.

4 Grate the frozen lard and place it back in the freezer (you'll be adding this later when we create layers in the dough).

5 While the dough is chilling, make the filling. Heat some oil in a large frying pan over medium heat, add the onion and carrot and cook for 2–3 minutes, then add the garlic, cover with the lid and cook for about 5 minutes until softened. Remove the lid and add the beef, smoked paprika, pepper and curry powder, then, using a potato masher, mash the meat as it cooks until smooth and evenly browned. Stir in the breadcrumbs, water, soy sauce, browning and salt to taste, then reduce the heat, re-cover and cook for about 10 minutes, stirring occasionally. Remove from the heat and let it cool completely.

6 Take the chilled pastry dough out of the fridge and place on a lightly floured surface. Roll out into a rectangle about ½ in (1 cm) thick and sprinkle the frozen grated lard evenly across the dough. Fold one-third of the dough towards the center, then fold the remaining third on top, like folding a letter. Rotate the dough 90 degrees and roll it out again to the same size. Repeat the folding process once more to create beautiful layers, then return the dough to the fridge and chill for 25 minutes. Repeat the folding process twice more to build up the layers.

7 When ready to assemble the patties, preheat your oven to 400°F (200°C) and line a baking sheet with parchment paper.

Continued overleaf

8 Roll out the dough into a large rectangle, about 20 in (50 cm) wide, and cut into 6–8 large squares or circles, depending on your preference. Spoon a generous amount of the beef filling onto one side of each dough piece, leaving a border around the edges. Fold the dough over the filling, pressing firmly around the edges to seal and making sure there's no air trapped inside. Using a fork, crimp the edges to securely seal. Brush with the egg wash.

9 Place the patties on the prepared baking sheet and pierce a couple of small holes in each to allow steam to escape. Bake for 25–30 minutes until the patties are golden brown and puffed up. Let the patties cool for 5–10 minutes before digging in— they'll be steaming hot and perfectly flaky!

TIP

The secret to flaky pastry is keeping everything cold. It is best to avoid using your hands directly on the cold butter and lard, as it can warm it up. If you do use your hands, hold them under cold running water first, then dry. Make sure your meat filling is cool before assembly—if it is still hot, you won't get crispy layers of pastry.

Sugar & Spice

Honey Jalapeño *Cornbread*

For some reason, cornbread just hasn't caught on in the UK, which is a shame because it's perfect for our weather—it is traditionally served with soup in cold, rainy weather. Sound familiar? To kick things up a notch, I've added jalapeños and Cheddar. Sure, it's not the traditional route, but sometimes breaking the rules makes things even better.

**Makes 12 large slices
or 24 small pieces**

1⅓ cups (250 g) fine yellow
  cornmeal
2 cups (250 g) self-rising flour
2 tsp baking powder
⅔ cup (125 g) granulated sugar
Generous ¾ cup (200 ml)
  buttermilk
2 eggs
1 cup (250 ml) milk
2½ oz (75 g) Cheddar, grated
2½ oz (75 g) Red Leicester (or
  Wisconsin Cheddar), grated
3 jalapeño chiles, diced
2 tbsp runny honey

1   Preheat your oven to 400°F (200°C) and grease an 8 × 12 in (20 × 30 cm) baking dish or line it with parchment paper.

2   In a large bowl, combine the cornmeal, flour, baking powder and sugar, making sure it is evenly mixed. In a separate bowl, whisk together the buttermilk, eggs and milk until well combined and homogeneous.

3   Gradually add the wet ingredients to the dry, stirring continuously to avoid lumps and until just combined; do not overmix. Fold in both cheeses and the chiles, ensuring they are evenly distributed.

4   Pour the batter into the prepared baking dish, spreading it evenly. Bake for 20–25 minutes until a toothpick inserted into the center comes out clean or with only a few moist crumbs. Remove from the oven and immediately pour the honey on top.

5   Allow to cool in the baking dish for about 10 minutes, then transfer to a wire rack to cool (if you can wait!). Cut the cornbread into small squares or large slices to serve.

TIP

Leftover cornbread can be kept in an airtight container in the fridge for up to 2 days.

Jerk Mushroom *Pasta*

If you love authentic food, hide your eyes from this one, it's not authentic but is still delicious. It's the perfect way to get your veggies in too. The Parmesan gives the sauce a rich, creamy texture and balances the spice from the jerk paste.

Loads of veggies means we can treat ourselves to an indulgent dessert, right? Vegan Crinkly Top Brownies (see page 198) coming up!

Serves 4

10½ oz (300 g) pasta of your choosing
Olive oil, for frying
1 red pepper, deseeded and sliced
1 yellow pepper, deseeded and sliced
1 red onion, sliced
4 garlic cloves, minced
1 lb 2 oz (500 g) Portobello mushrooms, sliced
2 tbsp jerk paste
1 tsp smoked paprika
½ tsp black pepper
1 tsp Old Bay Seasoning or all-purpose seasoning
2 cups (500 ml) coconut cream, plus extra if needed
1¾ oz (50 g) Parmesan, grated
Heaped 1 tbsp finely chopped fresh parsley (optional)
Salt

1 Begin by cooking your pasta in a large pot of salted boiling water according to the package instructions until al dente. Drain, reserving some of the pasta water in case the sauce needs loosening later. Set the pasta aside.

2 Meanwhile, heat a little of the oil in a large sauté pan over medium heat, add the red and yellow peppers and onion and cook for 5–7 minutes until the vegetables are softened and slightly caramelized. Stir in the garlic and mushrooms and cook for another 5–7 minutes until the mushrooms release their liquid and become golden brown.

3 Reduce the heat to medium–low and stir in the jerk paste, smoked paprika, pepper and Old Bay Seasoning, making sure the veggies are evenly coated. Pour in the coconut cream, stirring well to combine, then cook gently for 5–10 minutes until slightly thickened. If the sauce feels too thick, add a splash of the reserved pasta water or more coconut cream.

4 Add the Parmesan, stirring until it melts into the sauce. Toss in the cooked pasta, stirring until it is fully coated, and cook for a couple of minutes until heated through and it has absorbed the flavors, then sprinkle the parsley on top (if using).

FRIDAY NIGHT
Cravings

Mr. American *Fried Chicken*

Kentucky sure knows how to fry a chicken, and after a "top-secret" chat with the Colonel himself, he slipped me a hint about what goes into that finger-lickin' magic ... okay, I lied. The Colonel's recipe is still locked up pretty tight. But I swear, this chicken right here? It tastes so close, you'll be wondering if I've got a secret handshake with him after all.

You do need patience for this recipe, but the best things in life are worth waiting for. The buttermilk marinade not only adds flavor but also helps to tenderize the meat beautifully, resulting in some juicy chicken! And trust me, letting your marinated chicken come to room temperature before cooking is crucial (cold chicken will lower the oil temperature, meaning it cooks unevenly). By taking your time, you'll get perfectly cooked chicken.

Serves 3–4

6–8 chicken pieces (a mixture
    of thighs and drumsticks),
    skin on and bone in
Vegetable/sunflower oil,
    for deep-frying

For the marinade
1¼ cups (300 ml) buttermilk
2 tbsp smoked paprika
1½ tbsp garlic granules
1½ tbsp onion granules
2 tbsp white pepper

For the coating
3 cups (375 g) all-purpose flour
1 cup (100 g) cornstarch
1¾ oz (50 g) Cajun seasoning
1½ tbsp sugar
Heaped 1 tbsp fine salt
3½ tbsp smoked paprika
2½ tbsp garlic granules
2½ tbsp onion granules
1 tbsp ground black pepper
4 tbsp dried parsley
1 tbsp MSG (optional)

TIP
If you use a transparent bowl to mix your coating, you can easily check the bottom of the bowl to make sure everything is thoroughly combined.

1 First things first, put your chicken pieces into a large bowl or resealable plastic bag. In a separate bowl, whisk together all the marinade ingredients, then pour this tangy marinade over the chicken, making sure each piece is fully coated. Cover the bowl or seal the bag. Now, here's the key: let the chicken soak up all those flavors in the fridge for 3 hours.

2 While the chicken is marinating, grab a large, shallow bowl. Toss in all your coating ingredients and mix well until combined. Set aside.

3 When marinated, take the chicken out of the fridge and let it come to room temperature for 1 hour. Now for the fun part! Take your chicken, one piece at a time, and press it firmly into the coating mix, then really work in the mixture, making sure it sticks to every nook and cranny, until you have a thick, even coating (this will create those delightful ripples that make fried chicken irresistibly crispy). When all the chicken is coated, transfer the pieces to a wire rack and let them sit for 10 minutes. This allows the flour to be absorbed by the chicken, so it won't be as white when you fry it. When you see the flour starting to look less powdery, you're good to go!

4 Pour the oil into a large, deep pot to a depth of at least 1½ in (4 cm) and heat to 350°F (175°C). Working in batches to avoid overcrowding the pot and lowering the oil temperature, carefully place the chicken in the hot oil and fry for 12–15 minutes, turning occasionally, until golden brown and cooked through with an internal temperature of 170°F (75°C). Remove with a slotted spoon and drain on a wire rack placed over a baking sheet to drain any excess oil.

5 Let the chicken rest for a few minutes before serving—it'll stay juicy inside and perfectly crunchy on the outside.

Salt & Pepper *Fries*

If you're ordering Chinese food without salt and pepper fries, you're missing out! And once you make this recipe, you'll understand why—these taste just as amazing as salt and pepper fries from my local takeout place. And the best part? They're super easy on the wallet. Now you can enjoy those delicious flavors at home anytime. Personally, I prefer skin-on fries but you can peel the potatoes if you like.

Serves 4

6 large potatoes (like Yukon gold), about 2 lb 3 oz (1 kg) in total, washed
2 tbsp cornstarch
Sunflower oil (or any frying oil), for deep-frying
3½ tbsp unsalted butter
3 garlic cloves, minced
1 small onion, cut into chunks
2 scallions, sliced
1 red chile, sliced

For the salt and pepper seasoning
1 tsp white pepper
1 tsp Chinese five spice powder
1 tsp black pepper
1 tsp salt

1 First, slice a thin piece of the long side of both ends of your potatoes to create flat surfaces. Next, cut it into planks about ¾ in (2 cm) thick, depending on how thick you like your fries. Carefully stack these planks and slice them into sticks of the same thickness. Repeat with the remaining potatoes.

2 Put the potatoes into a bowl of iced water and allow to soak for 25–30 minutes to remove excess starch (this helps make your fries crispier). Drain the potatoes and pat dry with a clean tea towel or paper towels. Tip into a large bowl, add the cornstarch and toss until evenly coated (this step is crucial for achieving a crispy exterior).

3 Line a plate with paper towels. Heat the oil in a large, deep skillet or deep fryer to 350–375°F (175–190°C). Working in batches to avoid overcrowding the pan, carefully lower the potatoes into the hot oil and deep-fry for 10–15 minutes, depending on the thickness, until golden brown and crispy. Remove with a slotted spoon and drain on the lined plate.

4 Meanwhile, melt the butter in a large frying pan over medium heat, add the garlic and onion and sauté for a few minutes until fragrant and the onion begins to soften. Add the scallions and chile and cook for another minute or so, just until they start to soften but still retain some crunch.

5 In a separate small bowl, mix together the ingredients for your flavorful salt and pepper seasoning.

6 When all the fries are cooked, add them to the butter mixture in the pan and toss together until well coated in the mixture. Sprinkle over the salt and pepper seasoning and toss again, making sure the fries are generously and evenly coated.

7 Serve immediately, while hot and crispy.

Golden Arches *Fish*

The first time I tried this from the golden arches, I was already 23. It's my fiancé Liam's go-to order, so I figured it was about time I tried it myself to see what all the hype was about. It's good—but this homemade version knocks it out of the park!

Makes 4 fish sandwiches

4 skinless cod fillets
    (about 4½ oz/125 g each)
Vegetable oil, for frying
4 brioche buns, halved
4 large cheese slices

For the coatings
2 large eggs
1 tsp Dijon mustard
Heaped ¾ cup (100 g) all-
    purpose flour
1 tsp garlic granules
1 tsp black pepper
1 tsp salt
3 cups (150 g) panko
    breadcrumbs

For the tartar sauce
⅔ cup (150 g) mayonnaise
1¾ oz (50 g) pickles, cubed
1 tbsp lemon juice
½ tsp sugar
½ tsp onion granules
1 tsp black pepper
Small handful of fresh parsley
    and dill, finely chopped

1 First, make your tartar sauce. Put all the ingredients into a bowl and stir well until combined, then cover and refrigerate while you prepare the fish.

2 To prepare the coatings, put the eggs and Dijon mustard into a bowl and whisk together to form the wet mixture. Combine the flour, garlic granules, pepper and salt in a second bowl for the dry mix. Pour the panko breadcrumbs into a third bowl.

3 Pat the cod fillets dry with paper towels. Dip each fillet first into the dry mixture and then into the wet mixture, and finally coat in the breadcrumbs, ensuring an even coating on all sides.

4 Heat a generous amount of oil in a large frying pan over medium-high heat, add the fish fillets and cook for 3–4 minutes on each side until the crust is golden brown and the cod is cooked through with an internal temperature of 145°F (63°C). Remove from the pan and drain on a plate lined with paper towels.

5 Lightly toast the brioche buns in the frying pan and place a slice of cheese on the bottom half of each bun. Place the fried fish fillet on top, then add a generous dollop of your homemade tartar sauce. Top with the brioche lids and enjoy!

TIP
If you're feeling lazy you can always buy ready-made tartar sauce, but homemade does taste so much better!

Char Siu *BBQ Pork*

Let's be real—Chinese takeout is one of the best! If I'm not ordering black bean chicken with egg fried rice, it's char siu pork and roast duck, but only from one restaurant in London. I even tried to sweet-talk the recipe out of them (spoiler: no luck), but this version comes pretty close. So, go ahead, dig in and enjoy!

Serves 2–3

¼ cup (50 g) granulated sugar
2 tsp salt
1 tsp Chinese five spice powder
1 tsp white pepper
1 tsp onion granules
1 tbsp sesame oil
1 tbsp Shaoxing rice wine or white wine vinegar
1 tbsp dark soy sauce
1 tbsp oyster sauce
2 tbsp honey
3–4 tsp red food coloring (optional)
2 garlic cloves, minced
3 lb 5 oz (600 g) pork shoulder steaks (about 4 steaks)

1   In a small mixing bowl, combine all the ingredients except the pork and mix well until the sugar dissolves and the flavorful marinade is fully combined.

2   Place the pork steaks in a large dish or resealable plastic bag. Pour over the marinade, ensuring the meat is thoroughly coated on all sides. Cover the dish or seal the bag and refrigerate for at least 1 hour, or overnight for best results.

3   When ready to cook, preheat your oven to 400°F (200°C) and line a roasting pan with foil or parchment paper, then place a rack on top (this allows the air to circulate around the pork, ensuring crispy edges).

4   Pour about 1 cup (250 ml) of water into the pan beneath the rack (this helps prevent the pork fat from burning the pan and causing smoke as it drips during roasting). Place the marinated pork on the rack and reserve any leftover marinade.

5   Roast the pork for 10 minutes. Keep an eye on the water level in the pan and top it up if necessary. Remove the pork from the oven and, using a pastry brush, generously dab some of the remaining marinade over the pork, ensuring every part is coated. Turn over and repeat the process on the other side.

6   Return the pork to the oven and roast for another 10 minutes. Remove the pork once again and baste both sides with the marinade, then roast for an additional 10 minutes to allow the glaze to become sticky and caramelized. By now, the pork should be beautifully sticky and glossy, and have a slightly charred finish. Let the pork rest for a few minutes before slicing and serving.

TIP

Mix all the seasonings in a small bowl so you can test to make sure the combination is to your liking before adding it to the pork.

Cheeky Lemon & Herb *Chicken*

My favorite no-fuss restaurant to meet my friends is a popular Portuguese chicken restaurant, but sometimes we want to stay at home and save money, so I'll whip up this flavor-packed lemon and herb marinated chicken. Paired with piri-piri fries and Fanta with no ice, I'm basically dancing in the restaurant.

You've licked the sauce off the chicken—what next? Time for some Sticky Toffee Pudding Loaf with Miso Caramel (see page 180)!

Serves 4–5

3–3½ lb (1.3–1.6 kg) whole chicken
Salt and pepper

For the sauce
1 red pepper
2 African bird's eye chiles, deseeded
12 garlic cloves, roughly chopped
4 tsp white wine vinegar
⅓ cup (75 ml) olive oil
1 tsp paprika
2 sprigs of rosemary, leaves picked
1 oz (30 g) fresh parsley, chopped
2 lemons, juiced
⅓ cup (75 ml) Greek yogurt
1 tbsp salt

1   First, toss all your sauce ingredients into a blender and blend until you get a smooth, creamy mixture. If it looks a bit chunky, just scrape down the sides and give it another whizz to make sure everything is well combined. Taste a little of the sauce—if it needs a bit more punch, add some extra salt, pepper or chile flakes until it's just right for you.

2   Next, heat a large pot over medium heat, pour in your sauce and cook for 10–15 minutes, stirring occasionally, until it thickens up nicely. Transfer to a serving bowl or other heatproof container and let it cool slightly, then cover and put it in the fridge for a few hours (this helps the flavors really come together).

3   When you are ready to cook, preheat your oven to 425°F (220°C). Spatchcock your chicken (see page 38), season with salt and pepper and place in a roasting pan. Pour about half of your delicious sauce all over the chicken, then roast for 45 minutes to 1 hour, or until the chicken is fully cooked through and the juices run clear, basting the chicken every 10 minutes with the remaining sauce.

TIP

When it's cooled, move your chicken into an airtight container and refrigerate for up to 3 days. Leftovers work great on a bed of boiled sushi rice with bok choi or broccoli.

Cilantro *Rice*

Yes, there's everyday rice, but sometimes you crave something a little more special. This rice is bursting with flavor and takes your meal to the next level. Its vibrant green color adds a fresh, eye-catching appeal to any plate, making even the simplest dishes feel elevated. With every bite, you'll taste layers of deliciousness. Whether served alongside a main dish or as the star on its own, this rice is anything but ordinary.

Serves 3

1¼ cups (250 g) rice (any kind you prefer, although basmati works great)
6 garlic cloves, roughly chopped
1 tbsp salt
2 tbsp fresh cilantro
2 cups (500 ml) water

1 Give your rice a good rinse under cold water to remove excess starch (this helps make it fluffy and light when cooked).

2 Put the garlic, salt and fresh cilantro into a blender, then pour in the water and blend until smooth and vibrant green. The aroma will be incredible at this point!

3 Transfer the rice to a pot, pour over the garlic and cilantro mixture and stir to combine, ensuring the rice is fully submerged in the green liquid. Bring to a boil over medium heat, then reduce the heat to low, cover with a lid and cook gently for about 15 minutes, or until the rice has absorbed all the liquid.

4 Remove from the heat and let the rice sit, covered, for 5 minutes, then uncover and fluff up with a fork before serving.

TIP

If you have any leftover rice, don't let it go to waste. Put it in the fridge and the next day, it'll be perfect for whipping up a delicious batch of fried rice. Cold rice fries up beautifully, giving you that perfect texture. Check out my fried rice recipes on pages 104 and 122 for some inspiration.

Butter *Chicken*

This is one of my favorite meals. I can (and have) eaten this for a week straight. Mainly because it's so delicious, and the longer it stays in the fridge, the better the flavors meld. By day three, it's still a party in your mouth. Now, this does require a lot of spices but they are all so, so needed. Curry is essentially a really well-seasoned stew, so if you don't have the right seasoning, it won't taste the same.

Makes 4 hearty portions

For the marinated chicken

1 lb 12 oz (800 g) skinless, boneless chicken thighs, cut into bite-sized pieces
4 tbsp plain yogurt
8 garlic cloves, minced
1 in (2.5 cm) piece of ginger, minced
1 tsp salt
1 tsp ground turmeric
1 tsp ground coriander
1 tsp Kashmiri chile powder
2 tbsp vegetable oil
1 tbsp ghee

For the curry sauce

4 tbsp vegetable oil
2 tbsp ghee
1 cinnamon stick
3 cardamom pods
2 large white onions, sliced
1 tsp salt, plus extra to taste
2 frozen ginger and garlic cubes
3 tomatoes, halved
2 tbsp tomato paste
1 tsp ground turmeric
1 tsp ground cumin
1½ tsp ground coriander
1 tsp Kashmiri chile powder
3 tbsp cashews
1⅔–2 cups (400–450 ml) boiling water
1 tsp garam masala
2 tbsp dried fenugreek leaves
2 tbsp salted butter
3½ tbsp light cream
Heaped 1 tbsp finely chopped fresh cilantro

1   First, marinate the chicken. Put the chicken pieces into a bowl and add all the remaining ingredients, then cover and marinate for at least 1 hour, but preferably overnight.

2   Preheat your oven to 425°F (220°C) and line a baking sheet with parchment paper.

3   To start the curry sauce, heat the oil and ghee in a pot over medium heat, add the cinnamon sticks and cardamom pods and cook, stirring, for 30 seconds. Add the onions, a pinch of salt (this helps soften the onions) and the garlic and ginger cubes and cook, stirring, for 2 minutes. Cover with a lid and cook for 15–20 minutes until the onions are softened.

4   Meanwhile, put the marinated chicken on the lined baking sheet and bake for about 25 minutes until cooked through and charred.

5   Remove the lid from the onions, then carefully place the tomatoes, cut-side down, on top of the onions. Re-cover, reduce the heat to low and cook for another 10 minutes. Remove the lid again and break down the tomatoes using a spoon, then stir in the tomato paste and a splash of water and cook for a few minutes. Stir in the salt, turmeric, cumin, ground coriander, chile powder and cashews, then increase the heat to medium and cook for a few minutes, or until the oil separates. Add the boiling water and bring to a gentle bubble, then re-cover and cook for 10–12 minutes, until the oil rises to the surface.

6   Reduce the heat to low, then uncover and remove the cinnamon stick and cardamon pods. Carefully blend the sauce until smooth. Stir in the garam masala and fenugreek and cook gently for another 2 minutes. Stir in the butter until it melts, then add the cream and cooked chicken, stir together and cook gently for 4–5 minutes. Stir in the fresh cilantro and serve.

TIP

Kashmiri chile powder contains a dye that helps the color of the curry. It can be replaced with another chile powder if you can't find it.

Spicy Tofu *Saag*

If this is what Shrek's swamp is like, sign me up! The vibrant green color makes this dish irresistibly enticing, and it tastes just as amazing as it looks. Paired with crispy tofu, it's the perfect midweek meal—delicious, satisfying, and a total feast for the eyes.

Makes 4 hearty portions

1 lb (450 g) firm tofu, cut into
   bite-sized cubes
2 tbsp cornstarch
1 tsp salt

For the saag sauce
6 tbsp vegetable oil
2 bay leaves
½ cinnamon stick
1 tsp cumin seeds
3 cardamom pods
3 cloves
1 onion, sliced
1 tsp salt
2 frozen ginger and
   garlic cubes (or crush
   10 small garlic cloves with
   1 inch/2.5 cm fresh ginger
   in a mortar and pestle)
1 large tomato, halved
2 tsp ground coriander
1 tsp ground turmeric
2 thin green chiles, halved
9 oz (250 g) fresh spinach
½ cup (50 g) fresh cilantro
2 tbsp cashews
1 tbsp dried fenugreek leaves
3½ tbsp light cream

1. To make your saag sauce, heat the oil in a largepot over medium heat, then toss in the bay leaves, cinnamon stick, cumin seeds, cardamom pods and cloves. Give everything a stir and let the spices sizzle for a minute until fragrant. Add the onion and sprinkle in the salt, then stir together and cover with a lid. Reduce the heat and cook gently for 10 minutes until the onion is golden and soft (slow cooking will bring out its sweetness).

2. Remove the lid and toss in the ginger and garlic cubes, then carefully put the tomato cut-sides down on the onion mixture. Re-cover and cook for another 10 minutes until the tomatoes are soft. Remove the tomatoes and carefully peel off their skins, then return to the pot and mash together with the onion to form a chunky sauce.

3. Add the ground coriander, turmeric and green chiles and increase the heat to high, then re-cover and cook for 2–3 minutes until the spices really bloom. Reduce the heat again and add the spinach and fresh cilantro, along with a splash of water. Stir together, re-cover and cook for about 20 minutes, stirring occasionally to make sure the greens break down and blend in with the sauce.

4. Meanwhile, preheat your oven to 425°F (220°C) and grease a baking sheet with a little oil. Put the tofu into a bowl, sprinkle over the cornstarch and toss until lightly coated (this will give the tofu a crispy texture). Arrange the cubes on the greased pan and bake for 20 minutes until golden brown and crispy, turning them halfway through.

5. Uncover the spinach mixture and remove the bay leaves and whole spices. Transfer to a blender, add the cashews and blend until smooth and creamy. Pour the blended sauce back into the pot over low heat, stir in the fenugreek and cream and cook gently for about 10 minutes until the flavors meld.

6. Remove your tofu from the oven. Ladle the rich, creamy saag into bowls or onto a serving dish and top with the crispy tofu cubes.

TIP

Serve the crunchy tofu on the side—if not, it will get soggy in the sauce.

Chicken Kebabs with *Saffron Rice*

I have to admit, Turkish food wasn't always on my radar. Living close to a Turkish takeout place, I always passed by without a second thought—until my sister decided to order one day. And let me tell you, that was a game-changer. The aroma, the flavors—it was like a party in my mouth. Since then, I've been hooked and now find myself ordering every other week.

Now, saffron is one of those ingredients that can feel a bit fancy, but when bloomed properly, it's magic and boy does it season chicken great and give the rice its vibrant color. The yogurt combined with the lemon and lime juices in this recipe tenderize the chicken, ensuring it stays juicy and full of citrus flavors. I serve this with smoky, grilled tomatoes and peppers, which complement the chicken and rice beautifully.

Serves 3

¼ tsp saffron threads
1 cup (250 ml) warm water
3 lb 5 oz (600 g) skinless, boneless chicken thighs, cut into bite-sized pieces
1 large onion, sliced
1½ cups (300 g) rice
3 beefsteak tomatoes, halved
4 sweet green pointed peppers
Olive oil, for brushing

For the marinade
⅔ cup (150 g) plain yogurt
3½ tbsp olive oil
1 lemon, zested and juiced
1 lime, juiced
6 garlic cloves, minced
1 tsp black pepper
Salt

1 To extract the full flavor and color of the saffron, start by blooming it. Crush the saffron threads in a mortar and pestle, tip into a measuring cup, then pour in the warm water. Let the saffron soak for at least 10 minutes until it has released its vibrant color and flavor. You'll use this saffron water in both the chicken marinade and the saffron rice.

2 To make the marinade, put the yogurt, oil, lemon zest and juice and lime juice into a large bowl, then pour in 3½ tablespoons of the saffron water and whisk together. Add the garlic, pepper and a generous pinch of salt and stir well to combine.

3 Add the chicken and onion to the marinade and toss well, making sure they are evenly coated. Cover and let marinate in the fridge for at least 4 hours, but ideally overnight (the longer it marinates, the more tender and flavorful the chicken will be).

4 When you're ready to cook, heat your grill to a low and steady heat. Thread the marinated chicken pieces onto 4–5 skewers (see Tip overleaf), then place on the grill and cook slowly, turning them frequently to ensure even cooking and prevent them burning, until cooked through with an internal temperature of 170°F (75°C) in the thickest piece. Alternatively, preheat your oven to 350°F (180°C). Place the skewers on a baking pan and bake for 15 minutes, flipping them halfway through, then increase the temperature to 425°F (220°C) and cook for another 20 minutes, flipping halfway through, until cooked through.

Continued overleaf

5   Meanwhile, rinse the rice under cold water until the water runs clear. Add the rinsed rice to a large pot of salted boiling water and cook according to the package instructions until it's nearly done but still slightly firm. Drizzle the remaining saffron water over the rice, stirring gently to evenly distribute the saffron. Cover with a lid, reduce the heat to low and steam for 10–15 minutes until fully cooked and infused with saffron flavor.

6   While the kebabs and rice are cooking, brush the tomatoes and green peppers with a little olive oil, then place on the grill (you could also use a preheated hot grill pan) until they're slightly charred and tender.

7   Serve the juicy chicken kebabs with the fragrant saffron rice and grilled tomatoes and green peppers.

TIP

For best results, use metal skewers, since they heat up and cook the chicken from the inside out. If you're using wooden skewers, make sure to soak them in water for 30 minutes beforehand to prevent burning.

Friday Night Cravings

Happy it's Friday *Sesame Chicken Bites*

This restaurant was all the rage back in my heyday, although by the time you're reading this, they might have closed their doors. But trust me, that doesn't take away from the legendary Jack Daniel's Sesame Chicken Strips—the star of their menu. These crispy strips are perfectly balanced with a sweet and salty tang, while the Jack Daniel's adds a delicious warmth that takes the dish to the next level. Even if the place is gone, the memory of those chicken strips is forever!

Whenever I visited this restaurant, everyone went crazy for their cookie pies. Luckily I have a recipe that tastes even better (see page 226).

Makes 3–4 hearty servings

3 lb 5 oz (600 g) skinless, boneless chicken thighs (or breasts), cubed
8½ cups (2 liters) vegetable oil, for frying

For the dry coating
Heaped ¾ cup (100 g) all-purpose flour
2 cups (100 g) panko breadcrumbs
1½ tbsp white sesame seeds
1½ tbsp black sesame seeds
1 tsp white pepper
1 tsp garlic granules
1 tsp smoked paprika
1 tsp salt

For the egg wash
2 large eggs
1 tsp white pepper
1 tsp garlic granules
1 tsp smoked paprika
1 tsp salt

For the glaze
3 tbsp neutral oil
2 garlic cloves, minced
1 tbsp brown sugar
2 tsp chile flakes
6 tbsp Jack Daniel's whiskey
4 tbsp honey
3 tbsp barbecue sauce
4 tsp sesame seeds, plus extra for garnish (optional)
1 tsp garlic granules
2 tsp salt

1 In a large mixing bowl, combine all the dry coating ingredients, mixing well to evenly distribute the seasonings. To make the egg wash, in a separate bowl, beat together the eggs and seasonings.

2 Working with one piece of chicken at a time (see Tip), first dip it into the egg wash, ensuring it is fully coated, then transfer to the dry coating, tossing thoroughly in the mixture and pressing the coating gently onto the chicken to make sure it sticks.

3 Line a plate with paper towels. Heat the oil in a large frying pan over medium heat until it reaches about 350°F (175°C). Working in batches, carefully add the coated chicken bites to the hot oil and fry for 4–6 minutes until golden brown, crispy and cooked through, then transfer to the lined plate to drain.

4 While the chicken is frying, prepare the glaze. Heat a little oil in a pot over medium heat, add the garlic and sauté for about 1 minute until fragrant. Add the sugar and chile flakes, stirring until the sugar starts to dissolve. Stir in the whiskey, honey, barbecue sauce, sesame seeds, garlic granules and salt and bring to a boil, then reduce the heat and cook gently for 3–5 minutes until thickened into a glossy glaze.

5 Toss the crispy chicken bites in the warm whiskey glaze until fully coated. Sprinkle with extra sesame seeds to garnish, if desired, and serve hot.

TIP
When you are coating the chicken, you may be tempted to coat multiple pieces at a time, but I find the chicken doesn't get as well covered this way.

Garlic Parmesan *Fries*

These Garlic Parmesan Fries are everything I look for in a fry: crispy and garlicky on the outside and soft potato fluffiness on the inside. I love ordering these at restaurants but making them at home is even better. Personally, I prefer skin-on fries but you can peel the potatoes if you like.

Serves 4

6 large potatoes (like Yukon gold), about 2 lb 3 oz (1 kg), washed
2 tbsp cornstarch
8½ cups (2 liters) sunflower oil (or any frying oil), for deep-frying
3½ tbsp unsalted butter
1¾ oz (50 g) Parmesan, grated, plus extra for sprinkling
4 garlic cloves, minced
Heaped 1 tbsp finely chopped fresh parsley (optional), or 1 tsp dried parsley
Salt and pepper

1 First, slice a thin piece off the long side of both ends of your potatoes to create flat surfaces. Next, cut them into planks about ¾ in (2 cm) thick, depending on how thick you like your fries. Carefully stack these planks and slice them into sticks of the same thickness. Repeat with the remaining potatoes.

2 Put the potatoes into a bowl of iced water and allow to soak for 25–30 minutes to help remove excess starch (this makes your fries crispier). Drain the potatoes, then pat dry with a clean tea towel or paper towels. Tip into a large bowl, add the cornstarch and toss until evenly coated (this step is crucial for achieving a crispy exterior).

3 Line a plate with paper towels. Heat the oil in a large, deep frying pan or deep fryer to 350–375°F (175–190°C). Working in batches to avoid overcrowding the pan, carefully add the potatoes to the hot oil and deep-fry for 10–15 minutes, depending on the thickness, until the fries are golden brown and crispy. Remove with a slotted spoon and drain on the lined plate.

4 Meanwhile, melt the butter in a small saucepan, then remove from the heat. Add the Parmesan, garlic and parsley and mix together. Add a pinch of salt and pepper, then set the mixture aside.

5 While the fries are still hot, drizzle the melted butter mixture over them and sprinkle some extra Parmesan on top (the heat from the fries will help melt the cheese slightly).

Mango Habanero *Wings*

I'll be honest, I've never been one for spicy food—yes, even being African and all. When I visit my favorite popular wings restaurant that cannot legally be named, I always avoid anything too fiery. But my good friend Catherine came over and completely changed my mind when she developed her own recipe. A huge thanks to her for inspiring this tangy, wonderful sauce that I'm now obsessed with!

Serves 3

1 lb 2 oz (500 g) chicken wings
1 tbsp salt
1 onion, cubed
I head garlic, cloves peeled
2 sweet yellow peppers, deseeded and cubed
2 yellow habanero or Scotch bonnet chiles, deseeded
2½ cups (500 g) canned mango pulp
2 tbsp white wine vinegar
¼ cup (50 g) brown sugar
1 tbsp runny honey
1 tsp salt
1 tbsp chicken bouillon powder
1 tbsp cornstarch

1 Preheat your oven to 425°F (220°C).

2 Put the chicken wings onto a baking sheet and season them with the salt. Bake for 30–35 minutes until crispy and golden, flipping halfway through to ensure even cooking.

3 Put the veggies, mango pulp, vinegar, sugar, honey, salt and chicken bouillon powder into a blender or food processor and blend until smooth. Pour into a sauté pan and bring to a gentle bubble over medium heat. In a small cup, mix the cornstarch with 2 teaspoons of water to make a slurry, then stir it into your sauce, stirring continuously for a few minutes until the sauce thickens, then remove from the heat.

4 When the chicken wings are roasted to perfection, add to the mango habanero sauce and toss well, making sure each wing is thoroughly coated. Serve these spicy, tangy and sweet wings hot!

TIP

Storing leftover sauce in an airtight container in the fridge will help maintain its freshness for up to 2 weeks.

Chile *Cheeseburgers*

For me, the ultimate comfort food is a big, juicy burger, and I like mine with a little kick. These Chile Cheeseburgers bring just the right amount of heat—not overwhelming, but enough to make things interesting. But if you're not big on spice, don't worry! The sweetness from the honey balances everything out perfectly, so you get that savory, spicy and sweet combo in every bite.

Burgers are indulgent (as they should be), so freshen up dessert with some Boozy Mint Tiramisu (see page 201).

Makes 4 burgers

2 lb 3 oz (1 kg) 20% fat ground beef
2 scallions, chopped
2 garlic cloves, minced
8 slices American cheese
4 burger buns, halved
Salt, to taste

For the jammy chiles
2 red chiles, sliced into rings
2 green chiles, sliced into rings
2 tbsp brown sugar
2 tbsp honey
1 tbsp olive oil
1 tsp vinegar

For the burger sauce
⅔ cup (150 g) mayonnaise
4 tsp yellow mustard
1 tsp superfine sugar
½ tsp white wine vinegar
½ tsp paprika
½ tsp garlic granules
½ tsp onion granules
1¾ oz (50 g) pickles, cubed

1 In a large bowl, combine the beef, scallions and garlic, mixing gently to avoid overworking the meat (this helps keep the patties tender). Divide into 8 equal pieces, about 4½ oz (125 g) each, then shape each into a patty slightly larger than your buns (they will shrink when cooked). Set aside.

2 Next, make the jammy chiles. Heat all the ingredients in a pot over medium heat, stirring until the sugar dissolves and the mixture begins to bubble and caramelize. Reduce the heat to low and cook gently, stirring occasionally, for about 5 minutes, then continue to cook until the chiles are softened and the mixture thickens and is glossy and jammy. Remove from the heat and let cool.

3 To make the burger sauce, mix together the mayonnaise and yellow mustard in a small bowl until smooth. Add the sugar, vinegar, paprika, and garlic and onion granules, stirring until blended, then fold in the pickles. Adjust the seasoning to taste.

4 Preheat a broiler to high or heat a frying pan over high heat. Using a burger press, press each patty until slightly flattened with a crispy edge, but still thick enough to remain juicy when cooked, then sprinkle with a pinch of salt.

5 Cook the patties under the broiler or in the frying pan for 2–3 minutes on each side, melting a slice of cheese on each in the final minute of cooking. Remove from the broiler or pan and keep warm.

6 Lightly toast the burger buns under the broiler or in the pan until golden and crisp.

7 Spread a generous spoonful of burger sauce on the bottom half of each bun. Layer 2 patties on top, then add a spoonful of jammy chilies for a perfect balance of heat and sweetness. Top with the remaining bun and enjoy every bite of this flavor-packed burger!

Frying Pan *Spicy Pepperoni Pizza*

This recipe is a tribute to my younger sister, Funmi. Without fail, every time she visits, she orders a large pepperoni pizza with extra jalapeños and two (sometimes three!) garlic mayo sauces. So, it only makes sense to dedicate this recipe to her—although I doubt I'll ever convince her to stop ordering it! By making the pizza in a frying pan, you get that perfect restaurant-style crunchy base with a deliciously gooey, cheesy top.

Makes 3–4 medium pizzas

For the dough
¼ oz (7 g) envelope instant yeast
1¼ cups (300 ml) warm water
4 tsp olive oil
3½ cups (435 g) bread flour
1 tsp salt

For the sauce
2 tbsp olive oil, plus extra for frying
1 small onion, chopped
3 garlic cloves, sliced
2 cups (500 g) canned chopped tomatoes
2 tbsp tomato paste
1 bay leaf
2 tbsp dried oregano
Salt and pepper

For the toppings
Sliced pepperoni
Ready-grated mozzarella
Small bunch of basil
Sliced jalapeños from a jar

1 First, make your pizza dough. In a small bowl, combine the warm water and yeast and let it sit for a couple of minutes until the yeast starts to foam, then stir in the oil. In a large mixing bowl, combine the flour and salt. Gradually pour in the yeast mixture, stirring with a wooden spoon or your hands until the dough comes together.

2 Transfer the dough to a floured surface (the dough will be very wet, but withhold the urge to add more flour) and knead by hand for about 10 minutes until firm and smooth. Place in an oiled bowl, cover with a clean tea towel or plastic wrap and let it rise for 1–1½ hours.

3 Meanwhile, make the sauce. Heat the oil in a sauté pan over medium heat, add the onion and sauté for about 5 minutes until soft and translucent. Add the garlic and cook for another minute until fragrant. Stir in the chopped tomatoes, tomato paste and bay leaf, then reduce the heat to low and cook gently for 15–20 minutes, stirring occasionally. Add the oregano and season with salt and pepper to taste, then remove the bay leaf and set the sauce aside.

4 When the dough has risen, punch it down to release the air, then divide into 3 or 4 pieces based on the size of your frying pan. On a floured surface, roll out each piece of dough into a circle that will fit the size of an ovenproof frying pan, keeping the edges slightly thicker for a nice crust.

5 Preheat your broiler as high as it will go.

Continued overleaf

6   Heat a little oil in your frying pan over medium heat. Carefully
    place 1 pizza base into the hot pan and cook for 2–3 minutes,
    or until the bottom starts to get golden and crispy. Spread a
    generous layer of the sauce over the dough, then arrange some
    of your pepperoni, mozzarella, basil and jalapeños (or any other
    desired toppings) on top.

7   Transfer to the oven and bake for 8–10 minutes until the cheese
    is melted and bubbly and the crust is fully cooked. Carefully
    remove the frying pan from the oven (it will be very hot!),
    keeping the oven on. Remove the pizza from the pan and
    let cool slightly before slicing and serving.

8   Repeat steps 6 and 7 with the remaining dough and toppings.

TIP

This is the one time I'll recommend ready-grated mozzarella
because of its low moisture content—perfect for this method. But,
if you feel like grating your own, use a low-moisture mozzarella ball
for an even better result.

Sugar & Spice

Korean Fried *"Chkn"* Wings

Just because you're plant-based doesn't mean you have to miss out! When I went vegan for a year, these bad boys were my go-to. They're so addictive that before you know it, you've polished off an entire head of cauliflower—and you're not even sorry about it.

Addictive wings need an equally addictive dessert, so Vegan Crinkly-Top Brownies are waiting for you on page 198.

Serves 2

4¼ cups (1 liter) sunflower oil (or any frying oil), for frying
Heaped ¾ cup (100 g) all-purpose flour
2 tsp garlic granules
¼ tsp salt
½ tsp black pepper
Generous ¾ cup (200 ml) unsweetened plant-based milk, such as soy, oat or almond
1 cauliflower, cut into even bite-sized florets

For the gochujang sauce
4 tbsp gochujang paste
2 garlic cloves, minced
3½ tbsp soy sauce
2 tbsp honey
1 tbsp rice vinegar
1 tbsp sesame oil
1 tsp chile flakes

To garnish
Sesame seeds
Sliced scallions

1 Over high heat, heat your oil in a large pot until it reaches 350°F (175°C).

2 In a mixing bowl, combine the flour, garlic granules, salt and pepper. Gradually whisk in the plant-based milk until you have a smooth, lump-free batter thick enough to coat the cauliflower but still fluid enough to drip off slightly.

3 Working in batches, dip each cauliflower floret into the batter, ensuring it is fully coated. Let any excess batter drip off, then place the florets in the heated oil. Fry until they are golden brown and crispy.

4 Meanwhile, prepare the gochujang sauce. Combine all the ingredients in a small saucepan and bring to a gentle bubble over medium heat. Cook gently for 2–3 minutes, stirring constantly until the sauce thickens slightly and the flavors meld. Remove from the heat and set aside.

5 Place the cauliflower in a large mixing bowl. Pour over the gochujang sauce and toss gently, making sure the florets are evenly coated but taking care not to break them up.

6 Transfer the cauliflower to a serving platter, garnish with sesame seeds and scallion and serve.

Carne Asada *Tacos*

Orange juice, beer and beef? Sounds like madness, right? Trust me, you're about to experience a flavor explosion like never before. The first time I made this, I felt like the rat from *Ratatouille*—you know that scene where he's tasting grapes and cheese and there are fireworks and colors everywhere? Yeah, it's like that. The citrus juices—orange, lemon and lime—don't just pack a tangy punch, they tenderize the beef until it's practically melting in your mouth. Paired with jalapeño guac and the salty tang of feta, it's a match made in food heaven!

Tacos are the definition of grazing for dinner so we're staying on that journey with Air Fryer Chocolate Sprinkle Doughnuts (see page 168).

Makes 5 tacos

2 beef steaks (about 1 lb 2 oz/ 500 g in total)
5 mini tortillas
1 white onion, sliced
Fresh cilantro

For the marinade
2 oranges, juiced
1 lemon, juiced
3 tsp soy sauce
3 garlic cloves
1¼ cups (300 ml) beer
2 tsp onion granules
2 tsp chile flakes
2 tsp steak seasoning (optional)
2 tsp smoked paprika

For the guacamole
2 jalapeño chiles, halved and deseeded
½ onion, roughly chopped
5 garlic cloves, minced
handful of fresh cilantro
1 avocado
½ lime, juiced
3½ tbsp water
Salt

For the toppings
Crumbled feta
Diced pineapple
Diced onion
Diced tomatoes

1 In a large bowl or resealable bag, combine all the marinade ingredients and whisk together. Add the beef steaks, ensuring they're fully coated in the marinade. Cover the bowl or seal the bag and let it marinate in the fridge for at least 2 hours, but preferably overnight.

2 When you're ready to cook, make the guacamole. Put the chiles, onion, garlic and cilantro into a blender or food processor and pulse until combined. Halve the avocado, then remove the pit and scoop out the flesh. Add to the blender or food processor with the lime juice and water and season with salt to taste. Blend until smooth and creamy, adding a bit more water if needed to reach a silky consistency that's perfect for topping your tacos.

3 Preheat your broiler to high or heat a grill pan over medium–high heat. Remove the steaks from the marinade and allow any excess liquid to drip off. Pat the steaks dry with a paper towel (this helps them to get a great sear). Cook the steaks under the broiler or in the hot grill pan for 4–5 minutes on each side, depending on the thickness and desired level of doneness. You're looking for a good char on the outside while keeping the inside tender and juicy. Let rest for a few minutes before slicing.

4 Meanwhile, heat a dry skillet over medium heat, add a tortilla and warm through for about 30 seconds on each side, then remove from the pan and keep warm. Repeat with the remaining tortillas. Alternatively, place each tortilla directly on a gas flame for a few seconds to get a bit of char.

5 Slice the grilled steaks thinly against the grain for the most tender pieces of beef. To assemble the tacos, place a few slices of the meat on each tortilla. Add whichever toppings you like, as well as a spoonful of the guacamole and a sprinkle of cilantro.

Cheesy *Caramelized Onion Rolls*

This chapter features a host of restaurants that shall remain nameless, but trust me, this roll is uncannily similar to one from a certain famous British bakery chain that happens to share a name with my mate Gregg. Think Flaky, Cheesy Goodness. Now, because I can't help myself, I added a little twist—my secret ingredient? Red onion chutney! It brings just the right kick to this.

Makes 6 large rolls

2 puff pastry sheets
1 tbsp nigella seeds
1 tbsp sesame seeds
8 vegetarian sausages,
   skins removed
½ cup (150 g) store-bought
   caramelized red onion
   chutney
5 oz (150 g) Red Leicester (or
   Wisconsin Cheddar), grated
1 egg, beaten

1 Start by taking the pastry out of the fridge to allow it to come to room temperature (this makes it easier to work with). Preheat your oven to 425°F (210°C). Line a baking sheet with parchment paper. In a small bowl, combine the nigella seeds and sesame seeds and set aside.

2 Crumble the vegetarian sausages into a bowl, then add the chutney and cheese and mix together until well combined.

3 Unroll the pastry sheet on a lightly floured surface and cut in half lengthwise. Divide the sausage mixture into 2 portions and form each portion into a long strip, then lay a strip along the length of each sheet of pastry, leaving space along the edges to fold over. Fold the pastry over the filling, pressing down gently to seal, with the seam side facing down for a clean look.

4 Cut into smaller rolls of your preferred size—I cut each strip into 3 pieces, to make 6 rolls. Place seam-side down on the lined baking sheet and brush the tops with the beaten egg (this will give them a nice golden finish as they bake). Sprinkle the tops with the seed mixture for a bit of extra flavor and crunch.

5 Bake for 25–30 minutes until the pastry is golden brown and the filling is cooked through. Let it cool slightly before eating. Alternatively, cool completely, then store in an airtight container in the fridge for up to 5 days.

TIP

If you have stored your rolls and would like to serve them warm, place in an oven preheated to 400°F (200°C) for 5–7 minutes until they have regained their crispiness. Avoid microwaving—it will make them soggy and ruin that perfect flaky texture.

Cajun *Wedges*

Let's be real—oven-baked fries rarely live up to the deep-fried ones. But these? These are a game-changer. The spice mix brings serious flavor, and the butter? It's the secret weapon that makes them beautifully crisp and golden in the oven. The butter and tomato paste mixture adds richness and a slight tang to balance the spices.

Serves 4

4 large potatoes (like Yukon gold), washed and halved lengthwise
3½ tbsp unsalted butter
1 tsp tomato paste
1 small sprig of rosemary, plus extra leaves to garnish

For the Cajun seasoning
2 tbsp cornstarch
1 tsp paprika
1 tsp cayenne pepper
1 tsp garlic granules
1 tsp onion granules
1 tsp dried oregano
2 tsp salt

1 Preheat your oven to 425°F (220°C) and line a large baking sheet with parchment paper or lightly grease it.

2 To cut the potatoes into wedges, place each halved potato flat-side down on the chopping board, then cut at an angle from the center towards the edge, creating 3–4 thick wedges, keeping them an equal size so they cook evenly.

3 Put the potatoes into a large pot of cold water, bring to a boil and cook for 5–7 minutes until they just start to soften but are not fully cooked (this ensures the insides will be fluffy when roasted). Drain the wedges and let steam dry for a few minutes in the colander.

4 Meanwhile, in a large mixing bowl, combine all the ingredients for the Cajun seasoning. Toss the parboiled potato wedges in the mixture, making sure they are evenly coated.

5 Melt the butter in a small saucepan over low heat. Stir in the tomato paste and the rosemary sprig. Let the rosemary infuse for a couple of minutes, then remove the sprig and discard. Pour the butter mixture over the seasoned wedges, then toss gently to coat.

6 Arrange the wedges in a single layer in the lined pan, making sure they aren't touching so that they roast evenly and get crispy on all sides. Roast for 30–35 minutes until golden brown and crispy on the outside and soft and fluffy inside, turning them halfway through to ensure even browning.

7 Sprinkle the wedges with rosemary and a little extra salt, if needed. Serve hot.

TIP

There's no need to peel the potatoes—the skin adds great texture and the cornstarch will also help the wedges crisp up in the oven.

Sweet & Sour *Paneer*

The book's called *Sugar & Spice*, so of course, I had to include a sweet and sour recipe! This one's a winner, with crispy paneer adding a deliciously salty crunch that perfectly balances the flavors. It's a must-try!

Makes 4 hearty portions

1 lb (450 g) paneer, cubed
3 tbsp cornstarch
1 tbsp sesame oil
3 peppers (any color, but I like to use a variety), deseeded and cubed
2 carrots, sliced
7 oz (200 g) pineapple flesh, cubed
Sesame seeds or chopped scallions, to garnish
Steamed rice or noodles, to serve

For the sweet and sour sauce

½ cup (125 ml) white wine vinegar
¼ cup (50 g) white sugar
¼ cup (50 g) brown sugar
¼ cup (75 g) tomato ketchup
⅓ cup (75 ml) soy sauce
1 tsp chile powder
3 garlic cloves, minced

1   Preheat your oven to 425°F (220°C) and grease a baking sheet with oil. Put the paneer into a bowl, add 2 tablespoons of the cornstarch and toss together, making sure the cubes are evenly coated. Spread the paneer on the greased pan and bake for 15–20 minutes until golden and crispy, flipping the cubes halfway through.

2   Meanwhile, heat the sesame oil in a large sauté pan over medium heat, add the peppers and carrots and cook, stirring occasionally, until they soften slightly but still have a bit of crunch.

3   In a bowl, whisk together all the ingredients for the sauce, then adjust the seasoning to your taste, adding more soy sauce for saltiness or more sugar for sweetness. In a small cup, mix the remaining cornstarch with a little water to make a slurry, then stir into your sauce.

4   Pour the sauce over the sautéed veggies and stir until they are all coated, then cook gently for a few minutes until the sauce thickens and becomes glossy and sticky.

5   Remove your paneer from the oven and add it to the veggies, stirring gently until it is coated in the delicious sauce. Lastly, toss in the pineapple and stir it all together for a minute.

6   Serve your sweet and sour paneer hot, sprinkled with sesame seeds or scallions for extra crunch and with steamed rice or noodles on the side.

TIP

If you've never tried paneer, think of it as halloumi, but better— creamy, satisfying and oh-so-good! If you're after a higher protein option, feel free to swap it out or replace it with some chicken.

Kimchi *Fried Rice*

Kimchi is a relatively new addition to my palate, but let me tell you—I'm obsessed! Paired with gochujang paste, it's a flavor explosion. Kimchi is fermented cabbage, and it brings a tangy, slightly spicy kick that transforms even the simplest bowl of rice. It's a whole new flavor profile that I highly recommend diving into. Don't stress about that jar of gochujang sitting in your fridge—I've got more recipes to help you use it up (see pages 31 and 94)! Trust me, once you start, you'll find an excuse to add it to everything.

The onions add sweetness and depth, and the sesame oil adds a rich, nutty flavor that complements the kimchi beautifully. This dish is finished with fried eggs, the runny yolks adding another layer or richness and creaminess.

Makes 3 hearty portions

2 tbsp vegetable/sunflower oil
7 oz (200 g) canned Spam, diced (optional)
1 large onion, sliced
2 garlic cloves, minced
7 oz (200 g) kimchi, drained (reserve 1 tbsp of the liquid) and chopped
1 tsp gochujang paste
1 tbsp light soy sauce
2½ cups (500 g) cooked day-old rice (I prefer short grain for this recipe)
1 tbsp sesame oil
3 eggs
Salt

To serve

2 scallions, green and white parts separated, sliced
1 tsp sesame seeds

1 Heat your oil in a large skillet or wok over medium–high heat until hot but not smoking. If using, add the Spam and fry for 3–4 minutes until golden and crispy at the edges. Remove with a slotted spoon and set aside.

2 Add the onion to the hot pan or wok and sauté for 2–3 minutes until softened and slightly translucent. Next, add the garlic and sauté for another minute until fragrant, taking care not to burn it (it should just lightly toast in the oil). Stir in the kimchi and its reserved liquid and cook for 1–2 minutes until the kimchi has released its juices, then stir in the gochujang and light soy sauce until well incorporated into the mixture.

3 Gently break up any clumps in the day-old rice with a fork, then add to the pan or wok and stir through the kimchi mixture so that every grain is coated in the spicy sauce. Fry for 4–5 minutes, stirring frequently to prevent it sticking to the bottom of the pan.

4 If you have used Spam, add it back to the pan and stir into the rice. Heat through for another 2–3 minutes.

5 Finally, drizzle over the sesame oil and remove from the heat. Season to taste with salt.

6 Towards the end of the cooking time, heat a little oil in a frying pan and fry the eggs to your liking—sunny-side up works perfectly for this dish.

7 Divide the kimchi fried rice among 3 bowls and top each with a fried egg. Serve garnished with the scallions and sesame seeds.

— TIP

Start by prepping all the ingredients—having everything ready makes the cooking process much quicker and easier. Using day-old rice is important because it's a little drier, which helps it to fry without getting mushy.

Beef *Chow Mein*

Beef Chow Mein is downright dangerous if you ask me—it's just too good. Perfect for a midweek meal, it's so easy to polish off the whole thing without even realizing it. Good luck resisting ... I've lost that battle more times than I care to admit! The chow mein sauce that coats the noodles brings this whole dish together with rich, savory flavors.

A quick noodle dish needs a quick dessert, so try my Cookies & Cream Mug Cake on page 142.

Serves 2

2 tbsp vegetable oil
14 oz (400 g) thin-cut beef steak, thinly sliced against the grain
1 onion, halved and each piece cut into thirds
5 scallions, cut into thirds
5 oz (150 g) bean sprouts
½ green pepper, sliced (or any veggies you have in the fridge)
14 oz (400 g) cooked egg noodles

For the chow mein sauce

3½ tbsp sesame oil
3 garlic cloves
5 tsp kecap manis (sweet soy sauce), optional
2 tbsp dark soy sauce
4 tsp light soy sauce
1 tbsp MSG
1 tsp sugar
1 tsp salt

1 First, prepare the sauce. In a small bowl, mix together all the ingredients, stirring well until the sugar dissolves and the sauce is combined.

2 Heat a tablespoon of the oil in a large wok or frying pan over medium–high heat. When the oil is hot, working in batches to avoid overcrowding the pan, add the beef and stir-fry until browned and just cooked through. Remove from the pan and set aside.

3 In the same pan, add the rest of the oil if needed and toss in the onion. Stir-fry for a couple of minutes until it softens and begins to brown at the edges. Add the scallions, bean sprouts and green pepper and stir-fry for a few more minutes, keeping everything moving so the vegetables cook quickly and maintain a bit of crunch.

4 Add the cooked noodles and toss everything together, making sure the noodles are evenly mixed with the veggies. Pour over the sauce and stir well, ensuring that every strand of noodle is coated.

5 Return the beef to the pan and cook for a couple more minutes, tossing it through the noodles and veggies, to allow the flavors to meld and the beef to warm through.

6 Your beef chow mein is now ready to serve!

TIP

Cutting the steak against the grain keeps the meat tender and helps it cook evenly.

Puff Puff *(Bofrot)*

Puff puff is a beloved snack made of fried dough, enjoyed all across Africa. In Nigeria, we call it "puff puff," while in Ghana, it's known as "bofrot." I have such fond memories of waking up to the warm, comforting aroma of cinnamon and nutmeg filling the air, knowing it meant a relaxed Saturday morning and puff puff was on the way. These days, I might not have the luxury of waking up to ready-made treats, but with every bite of these, I'm transported right back to those blissful mornings!

Serves 3

2¾ cups (325 g) all-purpose flour
⅔ cup (135 g) sugar
¼ oz (7 g) envelope instant yeast
½ tsp ground cinnamon
½ tsp ground nutmeg
1 tsp vanilla paste
1 cup (240 ml) warm water
Vegetable/sunflower oil, for deep-frying
Sugar, cinnamon and nutmeg, for coating (optional; not traditional)

1 Start by combining the flour, sugar, yeast, cinnamon and nutmeg in a large mixing bowl. Give it a quick stir to evenly distribute the dry ingredients.

2 Stir the vanilla paste into the warm water in a measuring cup, then pour into the flour mixture. Mix everything together until you get a smooth, sticky dough—don't worry if it's very watery, that's how it should be.

3 Cover the bowl with a clean tea towel or plastic wrap and let the dough rise in a warm place for about 2 hours, or until doubled in size and bubbly.

4 When you're ready to cook the puff puff, heat a good amount of oil in a deep pot over medium heat. To check if the oil is hot enough, drop in a small piece of the dough—it should sizzle and float to the surface. Line a large plate with paper towels.

5 Using a spoon or your hands, scoop small portions of the dough, then carefully drop them into the hot oil, in batches, and deep-fry for a few minutes, turning them occasionally until golden brown and cooked through. Remove with a slotted spoon and drain on the lined plate to soak up any excess oil. Sprinkle with spiced sugar, if desired.

TIP

The trickiest part of these is getting the shape right, since it's a very wet batter. Only pros like my mom make the perfect ball so don't be intimidated if yours are a little lopsided.

Mom's Best *Jollof Rice*

My mom makes the best jollof! Growing up, I heard many battles in the age-old war between Nigerian and Ghanaian rice. The truth is, there is barely a difference between them—and luckily, I am both, so I don't need to pick a side anyway. Jollof rice is vibrant and aromatic—this one-pot wonder combines rice with a symphony of tomatoes, onions, peppers and a blend of spices. My mom makes this the best way, so enjoy her recipe.

Stay on your West African journey and pair this with my puff puff on page 110.

Serves 6

1 tbsp vegetable/sunflower oil
½ red onion, diced
3 tbsp tomato paste
1 tbsp fresh thyme
1 tsp ground ginger
1 tsp chile powder
1 tbsp garlic granules
1 tbsp all-purpose seasoning, plus extra to taste
1 tsp black pepper
3 bay leaves
1½ cups (300 g) easy-cook/parboiled long-grain rice
Salt, to taste

For the stock
1 lb 2 oz (500 g) lean beef chunks
4¼ cups (1 liter) warm water
½ red onion
2 garlic cloves
1 tsp all-purpose seasoning

For the tomato sauce
2 cups (500 g) canned chopped tomatoes
1 red pepper, halved, deseeded and chopped
1 Scotch bonnet chile
1 onion
3 garlic cloves

1   First, make the stock. Put all the ingredients into a large pot and bring to a boil. Cook for 1 hour, skimming off any impurities that rise to the surface.

2   Preheat your oven to 425°F (220°C). Remove the beef from the pot, reserving the stock, and put it into a baking dish. Roast for 25 minutes. Set aside.

3   Next, make the tomato sauce. Put all the ingredients into a blender and blend to a smooth paste. Set aside.

4   When ready to cook your rice, heat the oil in a sauté pan, add the onion and cook until softened. Add the tomato paste and cook for 2–3 minutes until caramelized. You should be able to see dark bits at the bottom of your pot—that is where the flavor comes from.

5   Add the spices and the bay leaves and cook until fragrant, then pour in your tomato sauce and cook for 30 minutes until thick.

6   Rinse the rice thoroughly until the water runs clear, then add it to the pot.

7   Measure out 3 cups (750 ml) of the reserved stock and add it to the rice, then add the beef and mix together thoroughly. Cover the pan with foil and a lid and cook the rice over low heat for about 1½ hours, or until the rice is fully cooked.

TIP
Once cooled down, transfer any leftover jollof rice to an airtight container and refrigerate for up to 3 days. Reheat with a few teaspoons of water.

Suya *Chicken*

Growing up, we didn't get to enjoy suya chicken often because my little sister is allergic to peanuts, and it's mostly a Nigerian dish. But whenever we went to hall parties (literally huge parties in community halls), it was always on the menu, and I absolutely loved it. Now that I'm living alone, I get to feast on it whenever I want, and it's just as delicious as I remember. If you're unsure where to get suya mix, look for it in African grocery stores or online.

Serves 3

3 lb 5 oz (600 g) skin-on boneless chicken thighs

3 tbsp suya mix, plus extra to serve

2 tbsp peanut oil

2 tsp smooth peanut butter

1 Put the chicken thighs into a bowl and add the suya mix, oil and peanut butter. Mix together until the chicken is well coated, then cover and refrigerate for at least 30 minutes, or up to 4 hours, to let the flavors develop.

2 Preheat your oven to 425°F (220°C). Line a baking pan with foil, and if you have a wire rack, place it on top (this helps the chicken cook evenly and get a nice char).

3 Arrange the marinated chicken thighs on the wire rack or directly on the foil-lined pan, spreading them out to ensure even cooking. Bake for 20–25 minutes, flipping the chicken halfway through, until it is cooked through and lightly charred.

4 To serve, cut the chicken into bite-sized pieces while it's still hot, then sprinkle a little extra suya spice mix over for an extra burst of flavor.

TIP

Typically, suya chicken is served hot with sliced onions, tomatoes and fresh lime wedges.

Corned Beef & Egg *Stew*

Growing up, I never thought much of this meal because it's made with such basic ingredients and uses canned corned beef. But over time, I've come to absolutely love it. There's something special about how a dish with such simple ingredients can be so hearty and satisfying. The corned beef gives a satisfying bite and as the eggs mix into the stew they add a rich texture—it's proof that comfort and flavor don't need to be complicated.

Makes 2–3 hearty servings

3 tbsp vegetable oil
1 large onion, chopped
2 garlic cloves, minced
1 Scotch bonnet chile, deseeded and sliced
2 tsp mild curry powder
1 tsp smoked paprika
1 tsp dried thyme
14 oz (400 g) can chopped tomatoes
12 oz (340 g) can corned beef, cut into chunks
3 eggs
Salt

1 Heat the oil in a large frying pan over medium heat, add the onion and sauté until softened and translucent. Add the garlic and chile and sauté until the aromas are released. Stir in the curry powder, smoked paprika and thyme and toast briefly to enhance their flavor.

2 Add the chopped tomatoes, cover with a lid and cook for 10–15 minutes, stirring occasionally, until the tomatoes break down and release their juices, creating a thick sauce.

3 Add the corned beef and stir gently so that it maintains some texture. Heat through until it melds with the tomato sauce and taste for seasoning (see Tip).

4 Make 3 small wells in the mixture, then crack the eggs directly into the pan, one into each well. Cook gently in the sauce until the eggs start to set but are still slightly runny, then gently stir into the stew, incorporating them without breaking them completely to keep some of their texture intact, before serving.

TIP

Taste the stew before adding any salt because the corned beef can already be quite salty. Add salt only if necessary.

Groundnut *Soup*

When it comes to African soups and stews, this one is hands-down one of my absolute favorites. It's hearty, delicious and made with just a handful of basic ingredients. For the best results, visit your local African or Indian butcher for smoked turkey, and don't forget to ask them to cut it into pieces—it'll save you a lot of time and effort in the kitchen.

Makes 6 hearty servings

2 lb 3 oz (1 kg) chicken pieces
1 tsp salt
1 tbsp black pepper
1¼–1½ lb (560–700 g) smoked turkey (ask your butcher to cut it into pieces)
2 cups (500 ml) water
3 bay leaves
2 tbsp chicken bouillon powder
2 large tomatoes

For the paste
1 large red onion
Thumb-sized piece of ginger
4 garlic cloves
1 Scotch bonnet chile

For the peanut butter sauce
1 cup (250 g) sugar-free peanut butter
2 tbsp tomato paste
2 cups (500 ml) boiling water

1 Start by preparing the paste base for the soup. Roughly chop the onion, ginger, garlic and chile, then put it into a food processor or blender and pulse until you get a chunky paste. If you're without a food processor, chop very finely by hand.

2 Season the chicken pieces with the salt and pepper, ensuring they are well coated, then put into a large pot with the smoked turkey pieces and the paste. Pour in the water, or just enough to cover the meat, then add the bay leaves and bouillon powder. Bring to a boil, then reduce the heat and cook gently for about 25 minutes, or until the chicken is tender and cooked through.

3 Meanwhile, in a heatproof bowl, mix together the peanut butter and tomato paste. Add the boiling water and stir until smooth and well blended. Transfer to a saucepan and cook over medium–high heat, whisking continuously, for 5–8 minutes until the oil starts to separate.

4 When your chicken and turkey are cooked, drop the whole tomatoes into the pot and let them soften for a few minutes. Remove the tomatoes with a slotted spoon, transfer to a blender and blend until smooth.

5 Add the peanut butter sauce and the blended tomatoes to the chicken and smoked turkey. Stir together thoroughly, ensuring the peanut sauce is fully incorporated into the soup. Increase the heat to high and cook for about 15 minutes, stirring occasionally, until you see more oil rise to the surface. Taste the soup and adjust the seasoning with salt, if needed.

TIP

This dish is traditionally served with fufu, which can be a bit tricky to master. If you're not up for the challenge, you can serve it with mashed potatoes instead—it's not exactly authentic, but it's a great substitute that still pairs beautifully with the rich flavors of the soup.

West African *Fried Rice*

I have a confession—I believe fried rice deserves just as much love as jollof rice, if not more. It's quicker, arguably tastier and definitely gets a boost in the "healthy" department (thanks to all those veggies, right?). Cooking the rice in chicken stock adds an extra depth of flavor that takes it up a notch. The sausage and shrimp? Totally optional, but that's how my mom always made it for us, and it's a tradition worth keeping.

This pairs perfectly with the Suya Chicken on page 116, served with plantain.

Serves 3–4

3 tbsp vegetable oil
1¼ cups (250 g) easy-cook/
parboiled long-grain rice
1 tsp garlic granules
1½ cups (350 ml) chicken
stock
1 onion, chopped
3 hot dogs, sliced
7 oz (200 g) raw jumbo shrimp,
peeled
1¾ cups (250 g) frozen
vegetables (a mix of peas,
corn and carrots)
1 chicken stock cube
2 tsp dried thyme
3 tsp hot curry powder
Salt

1 Heat 1½ tablespoons of the oil in a large saucepan. Check if it's hot enough by tossing in a few grains of rice—if they sizzle, you're good to go. Add all the rice and the garlic granules and toast, stirring, for 3–5 minutes until the rice starts to smell nutty. Pour in the stock, then reduce the heat, cover with a lid and cook gently for about 20–25 minutes, or until the rice is tender.

2 Meanwhile, heat a little more of the oil in a separate large pot, add the onion and cook until softened. Add the hot dogs and the jumbo shrimp. Cook until the shrimp just turn pink, then quickly remove the shrimp with a slotted spoon and set aside.

3 Add the frozen vegetables to the onion in the pot and cook for 3–5 minutes until any liquid has evaporated. Crumble in the chicken stock cube and add the thyme and curry powder, stirring well.

4 Transfer the cooked rice to the pot, mixing it thoroughly with the seasoned vegetables. Season with salt to taste, cover with a lid and reduce the heat to low. Cook for about 20–25 minutes to allow all the flavors to meld.

5 Fold the shrimp into the rice just before serving, for that final touch.

Yam & Egusi *Stew*

Yam and egusi is a classic Nigerian dish—rich, earthy and absolutely delicious! While some ingredients might not be in your usual supermarket, a visit to an African or international grocery store will have you sorted in no time.

Serves 3

14 oz (400 g) diced lean beef
1 tsp dried thyme
1 tsp salt
1 tsp ground ginger
1 bay leaf
5 tbsp palm oil
1 onion, chopped
1½ oz (40 g) dried whole crayfish
5 oz (150 g) ground egusi
3½ tbsp water
1 tsp chicken bouillon powder
1 tsp smoked paprika
5 oz (150 g) ugwu leaves, or spinach works well
½ small yam, peeled (see Tip) and cut into thick slices or cubes

1 Put the beef into a pot, add the thyme, salt, ginger and bay leaf, then pour in enough water to cover the meat. Bring to a boil, then reduce the heat and cook gently for about 30 minutes, or until the beef is tender.

2 Meanwhile, heat the palm oil in a large pot over medium heat, add the onion and the dried crayfish and cook until the onion has softened and the mixture becomes aromatic.

3 In a small bowl, combine the ground egusi with the water to form a thick paste. Drop spoonfuls of the paste into the onion and crayfish mixture and cook for 3 minutes without stirring, then gently stir the mixture (it will resemble thick scrambled eggs) and fry for another 2 minutes, stirring constantly, to develop the flavors.

4 Stir the cooked beef and its stock into the egusi mixture and season with the chicken bouillon powder and paprika, then add the ugwu leaves or spinach and mix in thoroughly. Cook gently for 10–15 minutes to allow the flavors to meld and the greens to soften.

5 While the stew is cooking, rinse the yam thoroughly under cold water to remove any excess starch. Put the pieces into a pot, cover with cold water and sprinkle in a pinch of salt. Bring the water to a boil over medium–high heat, then reduce the heat to medium and cook gently for 15–20 minutes until tender when pierced with a fork. Drain.

6 Serve the egusi stew with the yam.

TIP

You won't be able to use a vegetable peeler on the yam, so just slice off the skin, chop up the yam and boil, in a similar way to cooking potatoes.

Okra *Soup*

This is my mom's second favorite recipe (her first love is the Lemon & Blueberry Streusel Cake on page 178). She adores okra soup! The secret here is embracing the slime (see Tip)—yes, it's key! Don't let it scare you off; paired with pounded yam, it's absolutely divine.

Makes 4 hearty portions

1 lb 10 oz (750 g) diced beef
   (or any protein of choice)
1 tsp salt
1 tsp black pepper
2 tomatoes, halved
1 Scotch bonnet chile, halved
1 red onion, halved, then
   ½ roughly chopped and
   ½ finely diced
2 tbsp palm oil
1 chicken bouillon cube
   (I use Maggi)
1 tsp thyme
1 tsp smoked paprika
1 tsp all-purpose seasoning or
   chicken bouillon powder
1 lb 2 oz (500 g) okra
1 tsp baking soda

1   Start by preparing the beef. Place the diced beef in a pot, add a pinch of salt and black pepper, and pour in enough water to cover the meat. Bring it to a boil, then reduce the heat and cook gently for 20–30 minutes, skimming any impurities off the top. Once tender, set the beef aside, reserving the stock in the pot.

2   While the beef is cooking, use a blender or food processor to blend the tomatoes, Scotch bonnet, and the roughly chopped red onion until smooth, then set aside.

3   In a large pot, heat the palm oil over medium heat. Add the finely diced red onion and cook until it softens. Pour in the blended tomato mixture, add the bouillon cube, thyme, smoked paprika, and all-purpose seasoning or chicken bouillon. Stir everything together, cover with a lid, and let it cook on medium–low heat for about 15 minutes.

4   Once the tomato sauce is ready, add the cooked beef and let it cook gently on low heat while you prepare the okra.

5   Slice the okra into small circles. Place the beef stock in the pot over medium heat. Add the sliced okra and baking soda and let the okra cook for 5–10 minutes until it reaches a soft, slightly viscous texture.

6   Before adding the okra, taste the stew and adjust the seasonings if needed. Then, add the okra to the pot with the meat and tomato stew, stirring everything together to combine.

TIP

Don't add salt after you've added your okra to the stew—it will break down the slime!

Yam *Porridge*

Picture this: it's pitch black by 4 p.m. You sprinted to catch the bus after school, only to miss it—and did I mention it's pouring rain? After an hour-long journey home, you walk in to see a steaming bowl of this waiting for dinner. Absolute perfection. The yam, with its natural starchiness, thickens the sauce beautifully, making this dish the ultimate comfort food on a cold, rainy night.

Makes 4 hearty portions

1 red pepper, halved and
    deseeded
3 tomatoes, halved
1 Scotch bonnet chile, halved
3 tbsp palm oil
1 onion, chopped
1 tbsp chicken bouillon powder
2 tbsp ground crayfish
2 lb 3 oz (1 kg) yam, peeled,
    cut into large chunks and
    rinsed well

1 Put the red pepper, tomatoes and chile into a blender and blend until smooth. Set aside.

2 Heat the palm oil in a large pot over medium heat, add the onion and sauté until softened and fragrant. Pour in the red pepper mixture, then add the bouillon powder and ground crayfish and stir together. Cook gently for about 10 minutes, stirring occasionally, until the sauce thickens slightly and the flavors meld.

3 Add the yam, stirring well until coated in the sauce. Pour in enough water to just cover the yam chunks, then cover with a lid and cook for 20–25 minutes until the yam is soft and the sauce has thickened, stirring occasionally to prevent the mixture sticking to the bottom of the pot and ensure the yam is absorbing the flavors.

4 Before serving, mash some of the yam pieces slightly with a spoon into a creamy texture, leaving a few chunks for heartiness.

TIP

Aim to cut your yam into equal-sized pieces to ensure they cook evenly and are ready at the same time.

Shito *(West African Chile Oil)*

Confession time—I can't handle super spicy food, and this shito is HOT. It's a fiery little number, but it's also packed with so much flavor that it's worth the burn. Made with dried fish, onions, chile, garlic, and spices, shito is a rich, bold pepper sauce that's as delicious as it is intense.

If you love this, pair it with jollof rice (see page 114) or my West African Fried Rice (see page 122) for a kicker.

Makes 1 jar

¾ cup (175 ml) vegetable oil,
 plus extra if needed
3 onions, 1½ sliced and
 1½ roughly chopped
2½ oz (75 g) ginger, roughly
 chopped
1½ tsp chile flakes
1½ oz (40 g) dried whole
 crayfish
1¾ oz (50 g) ground shrimp
1 tsp chicken bouillon powder
1 tsp curry powder

1 Heat the oil in a large pot over medium heat, add the sliced onions and fry until they become golden brown and fragrant.

2 Meanwhile, put the roughly chopped onions into a blender, add the ginger and blend until smooth.

3 When the onions in the pot are golden, add the chile flakes and stir until they start to brown and release a rich aroma. Add the whole crayfish and ground shrimp, stirring until they are coated in the fragrant oil.

4 Next, pour in the onion and ginger mixture, then add the bouillon and curry powder. If the mixture looks too dry, add a bit more oil to ensure it all cooks evenly. Reduce the heat to low, then cook for about 1 hour, stirring occasionally, until the mixture becomes dark, rich and thick.

5 Allow it to cool slightly before storing. This will keep for 1 month in the fridge in a covered, clean jar.

Queeny's *Meat Pies*

This recipe is a tribute to my older sister Queeny, who, in my opinion, makes the absolute best meat pies. After much convincing (trust me, it wasn't easy), she finally shared her secrets. The dough here isn't a traditional flaky pastry—it's a bit thicker and denser, giving you that perfect homemade African pie that's hearty, comforting and deliciously authentic.

Makes 6–8 pies

For the meat filling
1 lb 2 oz (500 g) 20% fat ground beef
1 tsp dried thyme
1 tsp chicken bouillon powder
1 tsp curry powder
1 tsp black pepper
½ onion, chopped
1 small potato, diced
1 carrot, diced
¾ cup (100 g) frozen peas

For the dough
4 cups (500 g) all-purpose flour
1 tsp ground nutmeg
Salt
1 cup (250 g) margarine or butter, cut into small chunks
2 eggs
3½ tbsp milk
Beaten egg, for brushing

1 Start by making the filling. In a large pot, cook the beef, thyme, bouillon and curry powder and pepper over medium–high heat, stirring occasionally, until the meat is browned all over. Add the onion, cover with a lid and cook for about 2 minutes until it softens. Stir in the potato, carrot and peas and cook for another minute or two. Reduce the heat to low, re-cover and cook for about 10 minutes, stirring occasionally. Remove from the heat and let it cool to room temperature. This should take about 1 hour, giving you time to prepare the dough.

2 Meanwhile, to make the dough, combine the flour, nutmeg and a pinch of salt in a bowl or a stand mixer. Add the margarine or butter and mix in with your fingers or the mixer until it resembles a crumbly meal. Add the eggs and milk, mixing and kneading the dough with floured hands until it forms a smooth ball.

3 Divide the dough into 3 pieces, then flatten each into a thick round shape. Wrap them in plastic wrap and let rest at room temperature for about 30 minutes.

4 Preheat your oven to 400°F (200°C) and line a baking sheet with parchment paper.

Continued overleaf

5 On a floured surface, roll out the chilled dough to ⅛–¼ in (5 mm) thick, then cut out circles using a cereal bowl as a guide. Spoon a generous amount of the cooled filling onto one half of each circle, leaving a border around the edge. Fold the other half of the dough over the filling and press the edges together. Crimp the edges first with your fingers and then with the tip of a fork to securely seal.

6 Place the meat pies on the prepared baking sheet. Using a fork, pierce 2–3 small holes in the top of each pie to allow steam to escape, then brush the tops with the beaten egg for a golden finish. Bake for about 30 minutes, or until the pies are golden brown. Transfer to a wire rack to cool slightly before serving warm.

TIP

Traditionally this recipe makes quite a few pies but I've made a small-batch version here. Feel free to double it up and share these at parties or with friends or family. If you have some left over, they will keep in an airtight container in the fridge for up to 3 days.

Sugar & Spice

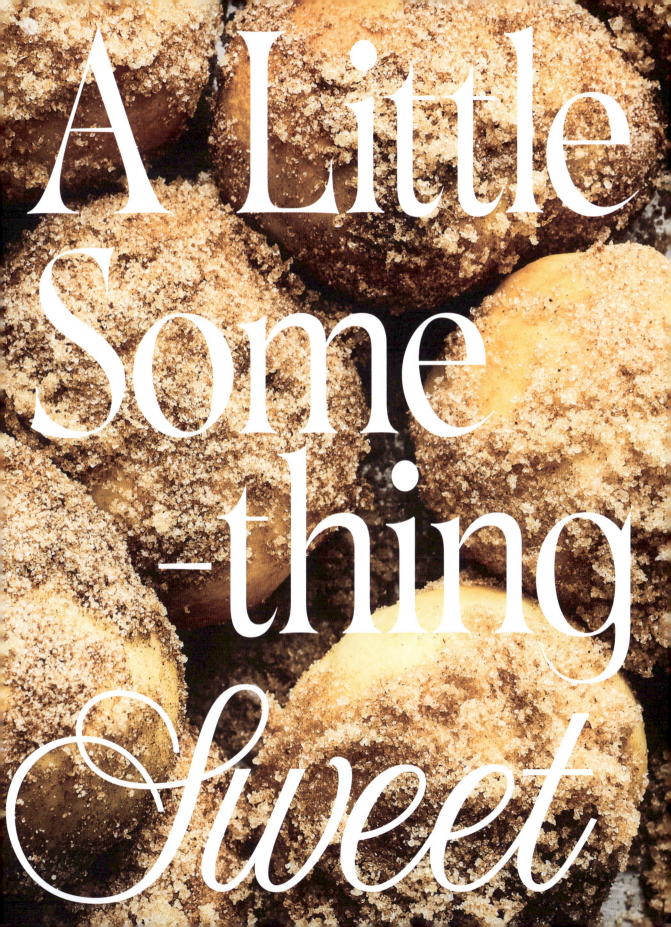

A Little Something Sweet

Single-Serve *Brownie Pie*

If you're craving a brownie, but don't feel like making a huge batch, then this single-serve brownie pie is just for you. I'm well known for my brownies as I used to sell them, but there's nothing better than a brownie just for yourself. Cooking these in a small dish means you get to eat them straight away and the gooeyness is delicious! I normally prefer my brownies cold but this brownie pie is best served warm. A total go-to for me.

Serves 1

3½ oz (100 g) dark chocolate,
    broken into pieces
5 tbsp (75 g) unsalted butter
½ cup (100 g) sugar
1 egg
6 tbsp (50 g) all-purpose flour

1   Preheat your oven to 400°F (200°C) and grease or line a small 6 in (15 cm) baking dish with parchment paper.

2   Melt the chocolate and butter together in a heatproof bowl set over a pot of gently bubbling water, ensuring the bowl doesn't touch the water (this prevents the chocolate from seizing) or in a microwave-safe bowl in the microwave, stirring until smooth. Let it cool slightly.

3   Stir the sugar into the chocolate mixture until combined, then add the egg. Fold in the flour until just combined, being careful not to overmix. Pour the batter into the prepared baking dish.

4   Bake for 12–15 minutes until the edges are set and the center is still slightly gooey. Allow to cool, then cut into 2 pieces and enjoy!

Single-Serve *Cinnamon Roll*

The moment there's a hint of chill in the air, I literally sprint to make this recipe. It's whipped up in minutes and tastes just like a cinnamon roll, but the best part? I don't have to share a single bite—it's all for me! The cardamom is totally optional, but trust me, it adds that extra kick of flavor that makes it even more irresistible. Perfect for those cozy days when you just need a warm, spiced treat all to yourself!

Serves 1

Generous ¾ cup (100 g) self-
  rising flour
⅓ cup (75 g) Greek yogurt

For the filling
3 tbsp (40 g) unsalted butter,
  softened
1 tbsp brown sugar
1 tsp ground cinnamon
½ tsp cardamom (optional)

For the glaze
Scant 1 cup (100 g)
  confectioners' sugar
1 tbsp milk
1 tsp vanilla paste

1 In a bowl, mix the flour and yogurt until it starts to come together to form a dough. Transfer to your work surface and continue mixing by hand, ensuring all the flour is fully incorporated and there are no dry pockets left. Let the dough rest for about 5 minutes (this helps it firm up and makes it easier to handle).

2 Meanwhile, combine the filling ingredients in a separate bowl until smooth. Set aside.

3 Preheat your air fryer to 350°F (180°C) and grease a small 4 in (10 cm) ovenproof dish or ramekin.

4 Roll out the dough on a lightly floured surface to a rectangle about 6 × 8 in (15 × 20 cm), but don't worry if it's not perfect—rustic is totally fine! Spread the cinnamon filling evenly over the dough. Using a sharp knife or a pizza cutter, cut the dough widthways into 3 equal strips. Roll the middle strip into a tight spiral, then wrap the other 2 strips around it, one at a time, to form a single, large cinnamon roll. Gently press the edges together to seal.

5 Put the assembled roll into the prepared dish or ramekin. Place in the air fryer and cook for 10 minutes, or until golden and cooked through.

6 Meanwhile, whisk together the confectioners' sugar, milk and vanilla paste in a bowl to form a smooth glaze.

7 Remove the cinnamon roll from the air fryer and drizzle the glaze generously over the top while still warm, letting it seep into all the layers. Serve immediately and enjoy while still warm.

Cookies & Cream *Mug Cake*

I'm all about a quick snack—although, for nutritional reasons, I probably shouldn't call this a snack. But hey, it's the easiest dessert in this book! Everything comes together in just one mug and in under 5 minutes. Perfect for when that sweet tooth strikes and you need instant satisfaction. For an extra indulgent twist, I highly recommend topping it off with a generous dollop of whipped cream. It takes this simple treat to a whole new level.

Serves 1

⅓ cup (40 g) self-rising flour
2 tbsp cocoa powder
1 tbsp sugar
2 tbsp vegetable oil
5 tbsp buttermilk
3 cookies and cream cookies
  (I use Oreos), crushed
1½ tbsp white chocolate chips
  (optional)

1   Sift the flour, cocoa powder and sugar into a microwave-safe mug large enough to hold the batter with some space for rising, to ensure there will be no lumps in your cake.

2   Pour in the oil and buttermilk and mix thoroughly until you have a smooth lump-free batter, then stir in the crushed cookies and chocolate chips until evenly distributed.

3   Place the mug in the microwave and cook on high for 1–1½ minutes, depending on the power of your microwave. Start checking at 1 minute to avoid overcooking it—if the cake has risen and looks set in the center, it's done.

4   Let the mug cake cool for a minute or two before enjoying it straight from the mug!

TIP

If you don't have buttermilk, add 1 tablespoon vinegar or lemon juice to the same quantity of milk and let it sit at room temperature for 5–15 minutes until it thickens and curdles.

Single-Serve *Strawberry Crisp*

For some reason, people seem to think cozy desserts are only meant for winter, but let me tell you—this one is perfect for summer too. It's light, refreshing and full of those comforting flavors we all love, no matter the season.

Serves 1

1¾ oz (50 g) strawberries, hulled and chopped
2 tbsp sugar
1 tsp cornstarch

For the topping
3½ tbsp (50 g) cold unsalted butter
6 tbsp (50 g) all-purpose flour
¼ cup (30 g) rolled oats
1 tbsp light brown sugar
2 tbsp sugar
Handful of walnuts, chopped
Handful of white chocolate chips

1   Preheat your oven to 400°F (200°C).

2   In a small bowl, mix together the strawberries, sugar and cornstarch until the fruit is well coated and the cornstarch has fully dissolved. Set aside.

3   For the topping, in another bowl, combine the butter, flour, oats and both sugars. Using your fingers, mix together until the mixture resembles coarse crumbs. Stir in the walnuts and chocolate chips.

4   Tip the strawberries into a small 4 in (10 cm) ramekin or ovenproof dish, then evenly sprinkle with the topping.

5   Bake for 15–20 minutes until golden brown and the strawberries are bubbling.

Almond Croissant *Cookies*

My viral almond croissant recipe took the internet by storm and you all went wild for them! They quickly became one of my most popular, most recreated recipes—and for good reason! These delightful treats are marzipan-based cookies, coated in crunchy almond flakes and dusted with confectioners' sugar. Here, I'm sharing a small-batch, improved version that's perfect for when you're craving a quick, indulgent treat!

Makes 6 cookies

¼ cup (50 g) light brown sugar
½ cup (100 g) white sugar
9 tbsp (135 g) unsalted butter, melted
1 egg yolk
1 tsp almond extract (optional)
1¼ cups (150 g) all-purpose flour
⅓ cup (30 g) ground almonds
½ cup (50 g) sliced almonds
Confectioners' sugar, to decorate

1 In a mixing bowl, mix together both of the sugars and the melted butter until well combined. Add the egg yolk and almond extract, then combine. Gradually add the flour and ground almonds until a dough forms.

2 Using a cookie scoop, portion the dough into 6 even-sized balls, or divide into 6 pieces, each weighing about 3 oz (85 g).

3 Next, spread the sliced almonds out on a plate. Roll the dough balls, one by one, in the almonds until they are completely covered, then shape into pucks and refrigerate for 25 minutes (this prevents your cookies from spreading excessively in the oven).

4 In the final 10 minutes of the chilling time, preheat your oven to 375°F (190°C) and line a baking sheet with parchment paper.

5 Transfer the dough pucks to the prepared baking sheet, leaving space between each one. Bake for 12–15 minutes until the edges are lightly golden.

6 Remove from the oven and allow the cookies to cool on the baking sheet for a few minutes, then transfer to a wire rack to cool completely. When cool, dust them with confectioners' sugar.

TIP

Store the cooled cookies in an airtight container at room temperature for up to 5 days. You can also freeze the cookies for longer storage. Simply place them in a freezer-safe container or bag and store them in the freezer for up to 2 months. Thaw at room temperature before serving.

No-Churn Strawberry Cheesecake *Ice Cream*

Ice cream is one of those things you forget about until you take a bite and think, why don't I eat this more often? I'm all about a chunky, funky scoop, so this one's loaded with real cheesecake pieces, juicy strawberries, and crumbly shortbread cookies. It's the kind of dessert that makes you fall in love with ice cream all over again.

Makes 2 pints (1 liter)

14 oz (400 g) strawberries, hulled and sliced
½ cup (50 g) sugar
2½ cups (600 ml) heavy cream
1 tbsp vanilla paste
14 oz (397 g) can condensed milk
7 oz (200 g) cheesecake, chopped into pieces
1¾ oz (50 g) shortbread cookies, chopped into pieces

1   First, put the strawberries and sugar into a pot and cook over medium heat for 3–5 minutes, stirring occasionally, until the strawberries break down slightly and the mixture thickens into a syrup, taking care not to overcook them. Leave to cool.

2   Using a hand-held electric mixer, whip the cream and vanilla paste in a large mixing bowl until stiff peaks form, but be careful not to over-whip (see Tip)—you want it light and fluffy. Gently fold in the condensed milk using a spatula until fully combined, making sure the mixture stays light and airy.

3   Next, take half of the cooled strawberry mixture and gently fold it into the cream mixture, but just enough to swirl the strawberries through and create distinct streaks, not to fully incorporate them.

4   Pour half of the cream mixture into a 4¼-cup (1-liter) freezer-safe container, then spoon over half of the remaining strawberries. Gently layer half of the cheesecake pieces and shortbread chunks on top and swirl in. Pour over the remaining cream mixture and top with the remaining cheesecake and shortbread. Finish with the remaining strawberries, swirling them on top for a beautiful finish.

5   Cover the container with a lid or plastic wrap and place in the freezer. Allow the ice cream to freeze for at least 6 hours, or overnight, until fully set.

TIP

It's really easy to over-whip heavy cream so when you feel the heavy cream start to thicken up, I like to take one beater off, it gives me more control and less of a chance of over-whipping.

Air Fryer *Cinnamon Bites*

With over 10 million views on TikTok, it's no surprise this recipe is a fan favorite—and I can see why! Ready in under 30 minutes, these treats are perfectly cinnamon-sugary and the ultimate pick-me-up after a long day. While the topping has more than just two ingredients, it's totally optional but trust me, it's so worth it!

Makes 30 bites

Heaped 1 cup (250 g) Greek
    yogurt
2¼ cups (275 g) self-rising flour
1 egg, beaten (optional)

For the topping (optional)
¼ cup (50 g) sugar
2 tbsp ground cinnamon
2 tbsp unsalted butter, melted

1 Start by mixing the yogurt and flour in a large bowl. Don't worry if the dough feels sticky at first, that's perfectly normal. Transfer the dough to your work surface and finish mixing it by hand, ensuring all the flour is fully incorporated and there are no dry pockets. Let the dough rest for about 10 minutes (this helps firm it up, making it easier to work with).

2 Divide the dough in half, then roll each piece into a long log. Using a knife, cut the dough into small pieces, then roll each one into a mini bite-sized ball (for uniformity, each doughnut should weigh about ½ oz/15 g, but you can eyeball it too).

3 Line your air fryer basket with parchment paper to prevent sticking, then preheat your air fryer to 400°F (200°C).

4 Place the doughnut balls in the air fryer, making sure to leave some space between them to allow for puffing up. If you want that golden finish, brush them with a little beaten egg before cooking. Cook for 5 minutes. Don't worry if they don't brown evenly—this can happen, but they'll still be delicious!

5 Meanwhile, if making the topping, put the sugar and cinnamon in a bowl and give it a good stir. When the doughnuts are ready, coat them in the melted butter, then dip each one into the cinnamon sugar, making sure to cover it completely.

6 The doughnuts are best eaten warm, with that perfect blend of buttery sweetness and cinnamon spice.

Caramelized Banana *French Toast*

Who says breakfast can't double as dessert? Especially when it's French toast! Add a cheeky splash of rum, and you've got yourself a real treat. I love making this for dinner parties—it comes together super fast and is the perfect way to refresh everyone's palate when they're already stuffed from the main course!

Serves 2

2 large eggs
⅓ cup (75 ml) milk
1 tsp vanilla paste
1 tsp ground cinnamon
2 tbsp unsalted butter
6 slices of brioche bread
Handful of walnuts, roughly
   chopped
Sea salt

For the banoffee topping
2½ tbsp unsalted butter
⅓ cup (65 g) brown sugar
3½ tbsp heavy cream
2 bananas, sliced
Splash of rum (optional)

1 Preheat your oven to 160°F (70°C).

2 To make the French toast, start by whisking together the eggs, milk, vanilla paste and cinnamon in a shallow dish until everything is well combined. Meanwhile, heat a large frying pan over medium heat and melt the butter until it starts to sizzle gently.

3 Dip each slice of brioche into the egg mixture, making sure it soaks for a few seconds on each side to absorbs all that delicious flavor. Place in the pan and cook for 2–3 minutes on each side until it turns beautifully golden brown and crispy. Transfer to a plate and keep it warm in the oven while you prepare the banoffee topping.

4 To make the topping, melt the butter in a clean frying pan over medium heat. Add the sugar and let it dissolve, watching as it begins to caramelize and turn a lovely deep color. Slowly pour in the cream, stirring constantly until the mixture becomes smooth and slightly thickened.

5 Add the bananas and cook for 1–2 minutes until they soften just a little. For a bit of extra indulgence, add a splash of rum to the sauce, if you like. When the topping is well blended and deliciously fragrant, remove from the heat.

6 To serve, spoon the warm banoffee topping generously over the French toast. Sprinkle some walnuts on top, and finish with a pinch of sea salt for that perfect balance of flavors.

TIP

Serve the French toast immediately. If there are any leftovers, store the banoffee sauce and bread separately in airtight containers in the fridge. They'll keep for up to 2 days.

Malted Milk *Banana Pudding*

I have a confession—I've never actually tried the world famous NYC banana pudding! But I'm sure this is exactly how it tastes. It's absolutely packed with banana goodness, so if you're not a fan, don't say I didn't warn you!

Serves 3

⅔ cup (150 ml) heavy cream
1 tsp vanilla extract
1 tbsp vanilla paste
4 tsp malted milk powder
9 oz (250 g) ready-made custard or vanilla pudding
10 oz (280 g) Madeira cake or vanilla pound cake cut into roughly ½ in (1 cm) thick slices
2–3 small ripe bananas, cut into thin rounds
3 malted milk cookies, crushed

1 Using a hand-held electric mixer, whip the cream, vanilla extract and paste and milk powder in a bowl until stiff peaks form, but be careful not to over-whip—you want it light and fluffy. Add the custard and whisk gently until smooth and well combined.

2 In your serving dish (such as a glass bowl or individual glasses), start with a layer of cake slices at the bottom. Spoon a layer of the custard cream mixture over the cake, spreading it evenly, then add a layer of banana slices. Repeat the layering if your dish allows, finishing with the custard cream.

3 For extra crunch and a lovely presentation, sprinkle the cookies on top.

4 Cover and refrigerate for about 30 minutes to allow the flavors to meld and the layers to set slightly.

Chocolate Chip *Air Fryer Cookies*

You are craving a chocolate chip cookie but the thought of whipping up my legendary Ultimate Chocolate Chip Cookie (see page 202) seems like a bit too much hard work? Well, there's a reason why I am the cookie queen— this is a single-serve chocolate chip cookie that's air fryer friendly. You're welcome in advance.

Makes 2–3 cookies (for one person)

7 tbsp (100 g) unsalted butter, melted
3 tbsp light brown sugar
3 tbsp sugar
1 egg yolk
1 tsp vanilla paste
Heaped ¾ cup (100 g) all-purpose flour
1 tbsp cornstarch (optional)
4 tbsp chocolate chips (feel free to add more)
Sea salt flakes

1   In a mixing bowl, combine the melted butter, both sugars, the egg yolk, vanilla paste, flour, cornstarch and chocolate chips and stir until you have a smooth and consistent cookie dough.

2   Scoop the cookie dough into 2 or 3 pieces and form into flat, round discs, then put into the freezer for 15 minutes until chilled.

3   Preheat the air fryer to 350°F (180°C), then line your air fryer basket with parchment paper.

4   Place the discs in the lined basket and cook for 12–15 minutes until golden brown on the outside and slightly soft in the center. Sprinkle with sea salt flakes and allow to cool for at least 15 minutes before serving.

TIP

Freezing the dough helps to ensure the cookies to spread evenly during cooking and results in the inside remaining super gooey when cooked.

Raspberry & White Chocolate *Cookies*

Raspberry and white chocolate truly is the ultimate combo—the tartness of the raspberries perfectly complements the creamy sweetness of the white chocolate. We're switching things up with these cookies by skipping the parchment paper and placing the dough directly onto a hot baking sheet. Since raspberries are packed with moisture, this technique helps eliminate any excess, giving us a perfectly chewy cookie with that ideal balance of flavors.

Makes 8 cookies

12 tbsp (170 g) unsalted butter, melted
⅔ cup (130 g) light brown sugar
¼ cup (50 g) sugar
1 large egg + 1 yolk
1 tsp vanilla paste
Scant 2 cups (225 g) all-purpose flour
¼ tsp baking soda
5 oz (150 g) white chocolate, chopped
¼ cup (70 g) frozen raspberries

1   In a large bowl, mix together the melted butter and both sugars until smooth and well combined. Add the egg, egg yolk and vanilla paste and mix thoroughly. Next, add the flour and baking soda, stirring until the dough just comes together. Gently fold in the white chocolate and raspberries, then refrigerate for 20 minutes until chilled.

2   Preheat your oven to 400°F (200°C) and place a baking pan in the oven to heat up.

3   Using a cookie scoop, portion the dough into 8 balls, each about 3 oz (90 g), and place on a tray or another baking sheet. Refrigerate again for another 10 minutes.

4   Remove the baking sheet from the oven, then carefully arrange the chilled cookie balls directly on the hot pan, leaving enough space for spreading. Bake for 10–12 minutes, or until the edges are slightly golden.

5   Remove the cookies from the oven and bang the pan down on the counter to release any trapped air (this makes the centers extra gooey and fudgy). Let the cookies cool on the baking sheet for at least 15 minutes, then transfer to a wire rack.

TIP

I've tested these cookies with fresh raspberries, raspberry jam and frozen raspberries—and frozen definitely give the best results with the perfect balance of flavor and texture (just make sure not to skip chilling the dough—the raspberries will release moisture if baked right away, leading to a messier cookie). That said, feel free to swap frozen with what you have on hand.

Honeycomb &
White Choc

Everything
But

Raspberry &
White Choc

Choc Chip
Airpyen

Everything-But *Cookies*

As the name suggests, this cookie has a bit of everything! Packed with pretzels, brownie batter, salted peanuts, mini peanut butter cups and more, it's a delicious medley of flavors and textures. The perfect balance of sweet and salty, crunchy and chewy makes this cookie a 10/10.

Makes 9 cookies

3½ oz (100 g) baking caramel

For the cookie dough
9 tbsp (125 g) unsalted butter, cubed
Scant ½ cup (75 g) light brown sugar
Scant ½ cup (75 g) sugar
1 egg
1⅔ cups (200 g) all-purpose flour
½ tsp baking soda
1 tsp baking powder
1 oz (25 g) pretzels, crushed
3 tbsp salted peanuts
2½ tbsp peanut butter chips
1¾ oz (50 g) mini peanut butter cups, halved

For the brownie batter
2¾ tbsp heavy cream
1¾ oz (50 g) dark chocolate, chopped
3 tbsp cocoa powder
2 tbsp unsalted butter

1 First, make the brown butter for the cookie dough (see page 14). Melt the butter in a saucepan over medium heat until it starts to foam. Continue to cook, swirling the pan occasionally, until it turns golden brown and releases a nutty aroma. Be careful not to burn it. Remove from the heat and let it cool for 20 minutes (if the dough is too warm by the time you add your mix-ins, the chocolate will melt into it).

2 When cooled, mix the cooled butter and both sugars in a large mixing bowl until well combined, then add your egg. Gradually add the flour, baking soda and baking powder, mixing until just combined. Gently fold in the remaining ingredients, making sure they are evenly distributed throughout the dough, then leave to rest while you make the brownie batter.

3 Next, make the brownie batter. Heat the cream in a small saucepan over medium heat until it begins to bubble gently—do not let it boil. Meanwhile, put the chocolate and cocoa powder into a heatproof and freezer-safe bowl. Pour the hot cream over the chocolate and let it sit for a minute until the chocolate begins to melt. Using a whisk or a spatula, gently stir until the chocolate is fully melted and the mixture is smooth and glossy. Stir in the butter until it is completely melted and incorporated. Transfer to the freezer and leave to cool for at least 30 minutes.

4 When ready to assemble, remove the brownie batter from the freezer, then dot teaspoons of the batter along the cookie dough, followed by teaspoons of the baking caramel (you may not need to use all the batter and caramel). Do not integrate them into the cookie dough—we are looking for chunks of caramel and brownie batter. Carefully mix the dough using your fingers so that you can feel the batter and caramel chunks and avoid squashing them too much.

5. Line a large baking sheet with parchment paper. Using a cookie scoop, portion your dough into 9 even-sized balls and place on the prepared baking sheet. Refrigerate for 10 minutes.

6. Preheat your oven to 425°F (220°C). Remove the cookies from the fridge, then squish into pucks. Reduce the oven temperature to 375°F (190°C) and bake for 12–15 minutes or until the edges are crispy, but the center is still gooey.

7. Depending on the amount of caramel added, your cookies may have spread a lot, so use a cup to gently reshape them while hot and soft, then enjoy.

TIP

We're cutting corners here by using ready-made caramel instead of making it, but it is really important to use baking caramel not regular runny caramel as that will ruin the texture of the cookies.

Honeycomb & Caramelized Chocolate *Cookies*

When I'm in the mood for something sweet, this cookie is exactly what I dream of. Imagine a rich brown butter dough, filled with crispy honeycomb bits and pockets of caramelized chocolate—it's like a flavor party in every bite! But don't worry, it's not too sweet. The brown butter adds a lovely, nutty richness, but it is the sprinkle of sea salt on top that is the secret magic tying everything together, balancing out the flavors and making each crunchy, chewy bite absolutely irresistible.

Makes 8 cookies

10 tbsp (150 g) unsalted butter, cubed
Scant ½ cup (75 g) superfine sugar
Scant ½ cup (75 g) light brown sugar
1 large egg
1½ cups (190 g) all-purpose flour
½ tsp baking powder
½ tsp baking soda
½ cup (100 g) caramel chocolate chunks or discs
Sprinkle of sea salt

For the honeycomb
½ cup (100 g) sugar
2 tbsp golden syrup (or light corn syrup)
½ tsp baking soda

TIP

When making the honeycomb make sure to line your pan with parchment paper in advance, as the honeycomb comes together fast. When done, fill the pot with hot water—the water will dissolve the sugar, making dish washing easier.

1 To make the honeycomb, first line a small baking sheet with parchment paper. Heat the sugar and golden syrup in a pot over medium heat, stirring occasionally, until the sugar dissolves and the mixture turns a golden amber color. Remove from the heat and quickly stir in the baking soda. It will expand like a science experiment so you will need to move quickly. Immediately pour the mixture into the lined pan and let it cool completely. Once hardened, break it into small pieces to mix into the cookie dough.

2 To make the cookies, first brown the butter (see page 14). Melt the butter in a saucepan over medium heat until it starts to foam. Continue to cook, stirring occasionally, until it turns golden brown and has a nutty aroma. Keep a close eye—you don't want it to burn! Remove from the heat and let it cool for 15–20 minutes.

3 Whisk both sugars in a large bowl, then add the cooled butter and mix until smooth. Crack in the egg and mix until well combined. In a separate bowl, combine the flour, baking powder and baking soda, then slowly incorporate into the wet mixture, stirring until a dough forms. Gently fold in three quarters of the honeycomb and the caramel chocolate, then refrigerate the mixture for about 30 minutes.

4 Line a baking sheet with parchment paper. Using a cookie scoop or spoon, portion the dough into 8 balls, each about 3 oz (90 g), and place on the prepared pan. Refrigerate again for at least 1 hour (this helps the flavors meld and prevents the cookies from spreading too much during baking).

5 When ready to bake, preheat your oven to 400°F (200°C). Bake the cookies for about 10 minutes until golden around the edges but slightly soft in the middle. If they've spread into funny shapes (it happens!), use a cup to gently reshape them while hot and soft.

6 Let the cookies cool on the baking sheet for at least 10 minutes, then transfer to a wire rack.

Ultimate Speculoos *White Hot Chocolate*

In those rare moments when I'm not cozied up with a cup of Earl Grey (you can find me raving about it on page 188), I'm treating myself to a mug or two of this silky speculoos goodness. It's the perfect companion for a chilly winter night in—pure comfort in a mug!

Makes 2–3 mugs

1 tbsp cornstarch
2½ cups (600 ml) milk
Generous ¾ cup (200 ml) heavy cream
1 cup (270 g) caramel chocolate chunks or discs
2 tbsp speculoos cookie butter (I use Lotus Biscoff)

1 In a small bowl, mix the cornstarch with a couple of tablespoons of the milk to make a smooth slurry. Set aside.

2 Heat the remaining milk and the cream in a saucepan over medium heat until it is warm but not boiling. Pour the cornstarch slurry into the warm milk mixture, whisking continuously to prevent lumps forming. Keep stirring until the mixture starts to thicken slightly.

3 Reduce the heat to low, add the chocolate and stir continuously until the chocolate is fully melted and the mixture is smooth. Add the speculoos cookie butter and continue stirring until it is fully incorporated and the mixture is smooth and hot. Be careful not to let it boil.

4 Pour the hot chocolate into mugs and serve immediately.

Cream Cheese & *Blueberry Doughnuts*

I'm absolutely obsessed with Bread Ahead doughnuts, but sadly, living outside of London means I can't just run to Borough Market for a fix. And let's be honest, making doughnuts at home takes forever, not to mention the whole deep-frying situation—who wants that mess? Enter my blueberry doughnut hack! They're quick, easy, and just as satisfying. Big shoutout to @seemagetsbaked for inspiring this speedy version that saves the day (and my doughnut cravings).

Makes 3 doughnuts

3 brioche buns
2½ tbsp unsalted butter, melted
3 tbsp sugar
⅓ cup (50 g) blueberries

For the cream cheese filling
½ cup (150 g) full-fat cream cheese, softened
3 tbsp superfine sugar
1 egg yolk
1 tbsp vanilla paste

1   Preheat your oven to 400°F (200°C).

2   First, make the filling. In a mixing bowl, blend the cream cheese, sugar, egg yolk and vanilla paste until smooth and well combined. Don't worry if there are still a few little chunks of cream cheese—they'll add some character. Set aside.

3   Carefully cut out a small hole in the top of each brioche bun, then press down to create a well in the center. Brush the tops and sides with the melted butter, then roll the buns in the sugar to give them a lovely, sweet coating.

4   Generously spoon the cream cheese mixture into each well, filling them up nicely. Scatter the blueberries over the top, letting them nestle into the creamy filling.

5   Bake for about 15 minutes, or until the buns are golden brown and the cream cheese filling is set to perfection.

TIP

Make sure to use brioche buns, the better quality the better—they taste amazing!

Air Fryer *Chocolate Sprinkle Doughnuts*

Whenever I eat doughnuts with sprinkles, I can't help but feel like Homer Simpson—totally in my happy place. These chocolate sprinkle doughnuts are no exception. They're fluffy, chocolatey, and topped with just the right amount of sparkle to leave you saying, mmm … doughnuts.

Makes 4 doughnuts

2 cups (250 g) self-rising flour
¼ cup (50 g) sugar
½ cup (25 g) cocoa powder
   (I use Dutch processed, see
   Tip on page 223, but regular
   works fine)
1 cup (250 g) Greek yogurt
Your favorite sprinkles,
   to decorate

For the chocolate ganache
1 oz (25 g) dark chocolate,
   broken into small pieces
2¾ tbsp heavy cream

1   First, make the ganache. Put the chocolate into a microwave-safe bowl. Heat the cream in a small saucepan until gently bubbling, then pour it over the chocolate. Let it sit for a minute, then stir until smooth and glossy. If the chocolate doesn't melt completely, you can microwave the mixture for 10–15 seconds and stir again. Set aside.

2   In a mixing bowl, combine the flour, sugar, cocoa powder and yogurt until a soft but not too sticky dough forms. Let it rest for about 10 minutes (this helps to firm it up and make it easier to handle).

3   Preheat your air fryer to 350°F (180°C).

4   Roll out the dough on a floured surface to about ½–¾ in (1–2 cm) thick. Using a doughnut cutter or 2 round cutters (one larger for the outer circle and one smaller for the inner circle), cut into 4 ring doughnuts. Don't worry if you don't have cutters; you can shape them by hand.

5   Lightly spray the air fryer basket with a bit of oil and place the doughnuts in the basket in a single layer, making sure they don't touch each other. Cook in the air fryer for 8–10 minutes until golden brown.

6   Remove from the air fryer and let cool slightly, then dip the tops into the chocolate ganache. Immediately sprinkle your favorite sprinkles over the top while the ganache is still wet.

Emergency Dessert *Chocolate Mousse*

I promised myself this book would be packed with real dessert recipes, and honestly, mousse didn't quite make the cut in my mind. But I'm a person for everyone, and I get it—not everyone wants to whip up a show-stopping dessert every time. So, this one's for you: the effortless dessert lover out there. It's perfect for when you want to impress guests (or just treat yourself), looking all fancy while secretly being a breeze to make. Plus, you can prepare it the day before and let it chill until you're ready to wow.

When the warm chocolate hits the cold cream some parts cool quickly, causing a stracciatella effect that enhances this dessert even more.

Makes 2

9 oz (250 g) dark chocolate, broken into small pieces
2 cups (500 ml) very cold heavy cream, plus extra to serve
Sea salt
Chocolate curls/shavings or raspberries, to decorate

1 Melt the chocolate in a heatproof bowl over a pot of gently bubbling water, ensuring the bowl doesn't touch the water (this prevents the chocolate from seizing) or in a microwave-safe bowl in the microwave in 20-second bursts, stirring after each interval, until smooth. Allow to cool slightly (it should be warm but not hot when mixed with the cream or it will ruin the texture of the mousse).

2 Using a hand-held electric mixer or stand mixer, whip the cold cream and a pinch of salt in a large mixing bowl until soft peaks form, but be careful not to over-whip—you want the mousse to be light and airy.

3 Mix a small amount of the whipped cream into the melted chocolate, then, using a spatula, gently fold the chocolate mixture into the remaining cream, taking care not to deflate the mixture. The goal is to keep it light and fluffy.

4 Spoon the mousse into 2 serving glasses or bowls. Cover and refrigerate for at least 2 hours, or until set.

5 Just before serving, top each mousse with more cream and decorate with chocolate curls or shavings, or even raspberries.

Brown Butter *Crispy Treats*

Who remembers those Rice Krispie treats you used to find in your lunchbox? Well, they're back—only this time, they've had a glow-up! Say hello to the new adult version with brown butter and toasted marshmallows. The brown butter brings a rich, nutty flavor, while the toasted marshmallows add a deep, caramelized goodness. It's the same treat you loved as a kid, but with a twist that'll make you wonder why you ever stopped making them!

**Makes 12 large or
24 small bites**

2¼ sticks (250 g) unsalted
  butter
1 lb (480 g) marshmallows
12 oz (350 g) box puffed rice
  cereal (I use Rice Krispies)

1 Line an 8 × 12 in (20 × 30 cm) baking dish with parchment paper, leaving an overhang on all sides for easy removal.

2 Melt the butter in a large pot over medium heat until it starts to foam. Continue to cook for 5–7 minutes, swirling the pan occasionally, until it turns golden brown and releases a nutty aroma. Keep a close eye on it—you don't want it to burn!

3 Reduce the heat to low, add the marshmallows and stir continuously until they are melted and start to toast slightly (they will turn a light golden brown and develop a caramelized flavor).

4 Remove from the heat and stir in the puffed rice cereal, working quickly to prevent the marshmallows from starting to set, until the cereal is evenly coated with the marshmallow mixture. Transfer to the prepared baking dish and press the mixture down evenly with a buttered spatula or piece of parchment paper.

5 Allow to cool at room temperature for at least 30 minutes, or until set. Lift out of the dish using the paper overhang and cut into large or small squares.

TIP

Avoid using high heat when you brown the butter, as this will burn the milk solids.

Blueberry & Rosemary *Muffins*

Whenever I'm in the grocery store hunting for a sweet treat, it usually comes down to two things: blueberry muffins or triple chocolate muffins. Nine times out of ten, I'm all about the triple chocolate indulgence. But when I'm in my "healthy era," blueberry takes the win because it's one of my five a day, right? These, however, aren't your average blueberry muffins—they've been taken up a notch with a drizzle of rosemary-infused syrup for a sweet, herbaceous twist. A perfect small portion treat and one of your five a day (I think!).

Makes 6 muffins

3½ tbsp sunflower oil
3 tbsp (40 g) unsalted butter, melted
⅓ cup (75 ml) milk
1 egg
1¼ cups (150 g) self-rising flour
½ cup (90 g) sugar
½ tsp baking soda
⅓ cup (50 g) blueberries

For the rosemary syrup
3½ tbsp water
¼ cup (50 g) sugar
1 small sprig of rosemary
(2–3 in/5–6 cm long)

1 Preheat your oven to 400°F (200°C) and line a muffin pan with paper liners, spacing them out in the pan (this will give optimum rise).

2 Whisk together the oil, melted butter, milk and egg in a bowl until smooth. In a separate bowl, whisk together the flour, sugar, baking soda and blueberries (this helps to prevent the fruit from sinking when baked). Gradually fold the dry ingredients into the wet ingredients until just combined.

3 Fill each muffin liner about two-thirds full with the batter. Bake for 20–25 minutes until a toothpick inserted into the centers comes out clean.

4 Meanwhile, make your rosemary syrup. Heat the water and sugar in a small saucepan over medium heat, stirring until the sugar dissolves. Add the rosemary sprig and cook gently for 5 minutes. Remove from the heat and let the syrup cool slightly (it should not be hot to touch). Strain into a pitcher and discard the rosemary.

5 Remove the muffins from the oven and allow to cool slightly, then drizzle with the rosemary syrup.

TIP

Do not overmix the batter as it can make your muffins tough. If you see a few streaks of flour, that's okay!

Desserts to Impress

Lemon & Blueberry *Streusel Cake*

I absolutely *love* blueberries—so much so that I've included a few blueberry recipes in this book! This particular cake is a family favorite. It's not overly sweet, and there's no buttercream, but it's still incredibly moist and delicious. Essentially, it's like a giant blueberry muffin. It's also perfect for gifting since it requires no frosting and is easy to transport.

Makes 8 slices

1½ cups (180 g) self-rising flour
½ tsp baking powder
½ tsp salt
3½ tbsp unsalted butter, melted
3½ tbsp vegetable oil
¾ cup (150 g) sugar (preferably superfine)
2 eggs
1 tsp vanilla extract
1 tsp lemon extract
½ cup (120 ml) milk

For the blueberries
¾ cup (125 g) blueberries
½ lemon, juiced
1 tbsp flour

For the streusel
⅓ cup (65 g) sugar
⅔ cup (80 g) all-purpose flour
3 tbsp (45 g) unsalted butter, melted, plus extra if needed

1 In a small bowl, toss together the blueberries, lemon juice and flour (the flour helps prevent them sinking to the bottom of the cake). Set aside.

2 Next, make the streusel for the top of the cake. In another small bowl, mix together the sugar and flour. Add the melted butter, then mix with a fork until it forms a crumbly texture. When you press it together it should form a dough but still crumble easily. If your mixture is too dry, add more melted butter. Set aside.

3 Preheat your oven to 400°F (200°C) and grease an 8 in (20 cm) round or square cake pan.

4 Sift the flour, baking powder and salt into a bowl. In a separate large bowl, whisk together the melted butter, oil and sugar until smooth. Add the eggs, one at a time, beating well after each addition. Mix in the vanilla extract, lemon extract and milk, then stir in the flour mixture until combined, taking care not to overmix (this can make the cake dense). Gently fold in half of the blueberries, being careful not to crush them.

5 Pour the batter into your prepared cake pan and spread it out evenly. Sprinkle the streusel topping and remaining blueberries evenly over the batter. Bake for 60–65 minutes until a toothpick inserted into the center comes out clean, the streusel is golden brown and the cake has risen beautifully.

6 Remove from the oven and allow the cake to cool in the pan for about 10 minutes, then transfer it to a wire rack to cool completely.

TIP

If there's any cake left (lucky you!), place it in an airtight container or wrap it tightly with plastic wrap. Store it in the fridge and enjoy within 2–3 days for the best freshness and flavor. Or you can break it up and add it to my ice cream on page 149.

Sticky Toffee Pudding Loaf
with Miso Caramel

This isn't your ordinary sticky toffee pudding—it's rich, moist and infused with deep, warm caramel flavors from the dark brown sugar and treacle, with a date paste that gives this cake its signature toffee-like sweetness. The nutmeg adds a subtle warmth that ties everything together, but the real star here? The miso caramel sauce. Miso might seem like a strange addition to caramel, but trust me, it brings a subtle savory note that balances the sweetness beautifully and takes this dessert to a whole new level. You'll be hooked!

Makes 1 loaf

4½ oz (125 g) dates, pitted and chopped
½ cup (125 ml) milk, warmed
3½ tbsp unsalted butter, softened
3½ tbsp molasses
2 eggs
½ cup (110 g) dark brown sugar
1⅔ cups (200 g) self-rising flour
1 tsp baking powder
1 tsp baking soda
¾ tsp ground nutmeg
¾ tsp ground cinnamon

For the miso caramel sauce
5 tbsp (75 g) unsalted butter
Scant ½ cup (75 g) dark brown sugar
2 tbsp light molasses
1 tsp vanilla extract
⅔ cup (150 ml) heavy cream
1 tbsp white miso paste

1 First things first. Preheat your oven to 400°F (200°C) and grease a 9½ x 5 in (900 g) loaf pan or line it with parchment paper.

2 Put the dates into a heatproof bowl, pour over the hot milk and let them soak for about 10 minutes until softened, then mash with a fork into a chunky, sticky paste.

3 Now, onto the batter. In a large mixing bowl, beat together the butter and molasses until smooth. Add the eggs, one by one, beating well after each addition (this helps create a fluffy texture). Add the sugar and stir until the mixture is smooth and creamy. In a separate bowl, sift together the remaining dry ingredients, then gently fold into the wet mixture—don't overmix or you'll lose that light, airy texture we're aiming for. Finally, fold in your date paste until evenly distributed through the batter.

4 Pour the batter into your prepared pan and smooth the top. Bake for 40–45 minutes until a skewer poked into the center comes out clean and the top is a beautiful golden brown.

5 Meanwhile, make the glorious miso caramel sauce. Melt the butter in a saucepan over medium heat, then add the sugar and molasses, stirring constantly until the sugar fully dissolves and the mixture is smooth and glossy. Add the vanilla extract and cream, stirring constantly, until the sauce thickens up a bit—this should only take a few minutes. And here's where the magic happens—remove from the heat and stir in the miso.

6 By now, your loaf should be ready. Let it cool in the pan for a few minutes, then transfer to a wire rack. To serve, slice the loaf and drizzle the warm miso caramel sauce generously over each slice. You can even pour some of the sauce over the whole loaf, letting it soak in for an extra sticky, decadent treat.

TIP

If you don't have blackstrap molasses, light molasses or British golden syrup is a good alternative.

Banana Bread *Cinnamon Rolls*

I know what you're thinking—cinnamon rolls are already perfect, so why add bananas? But trust me, this twist is a game-changer. They take these rolls to a whole new level, adding an incredible depth of flavor and keeping the filling moist and gooey, which makes them absolutely irresistible. Just wait until you catch a whiff while these beauties are baking! The brown butter cream cheese frosting that perfectly complements the banana and cinnamon is the final touch that makes them truly unforgettable. Get ready to have your mind blown!

Makes 12–16 cinnamon rolls

For the dough
Generous 1 cup (280 ml) milk
2 x ¼ oz (7 g) envelopes rapid-rise instant yeast
¼ cup (50 g) sugar (preferably superfine)
2 eggs
1 small ripe banana, mashed
5 tbsp (70 g) unsalted butter, melted
6¼ cups (750 g) self-rising flour
1 tsp salt

For the cinnamon filling
2¼ sticks (250 g) unsalted butter, softened not melted
Scant 1 cup (175 g) light brown sugar
2 tbsp ground cinnamon
1 small ripe banana, mashed

For the cream cheese frosting
7 tbsp (100 g) unsalted butter
Scant 1 cup (200 g) cream cheese
2⅔ cups (300 g) confectioners' sugar

1 Begin by warming your milk for the dough in a microwave-safe bowl in the microwave until it's like a warm bath—comfortably warm but not hot.

2 Transfer the warm milk to the bowl of your stand mixer fitted with the paddle attachment and sprinkle the yeast over the top. Let this sit for about 10 minutes until it becomes frothy (this means the yeast is activated and ready to work its magic). Next, add the sugar, eggs, banana and melted butter and mix together until well combined. Add the flour and a pinch of salt and beat until a dough begins to form.

3 Switch to the dough hook attachment and knead the dough on medium speed for about 8 minutes until it forms a slightly sticky and smooth elastic ball.

4 If you don't have a stand mixer, follow step 2 using a mixing bowl and a wooden spoon. At step 3, knead the dough by hand on a well-floured surface for 8–10 minutes.

5 Transfer the dough to a well-oiled bowl, cover with plastic wrap and a warm, clean tea towel and let rise in a warm place for 1–1½ hours until it has doubled in size.

6 It's now time to make the delicious cinnamon filling. Mix together all the ingredients in a mixing bowl until you have a smooth, spreadable paste. It's essential to make sure the butter is softened and not melted; if too gloopy, it can affect your cinnamon rolls. The banana in the filling adds an extra layer of flavor and keeps the filling moist and gooey.

Continued overleaf

7 When the dough has risen, transfer it to a well-floured surface and roll out to a large rectangle, ⅛–¼ in (5 mm) thick, keeping the edges as straight as possible (but don't worry if it's not perfect). Spread the filling evenly over the dough, making sure to reach all the edges, then starting from a long edge, tightly roll into a log. Trim about 1 in (2.5 cm) at each end if necessary to ensure neat edges and that every piece is packed with filling.

8 Grease an 8 × 12 in (20 × 30 cm) baking pan. Using a sharp serrated knife or, even better, unflavored dental floss, cut the log into about 12 equal pieces about 1 in (2.5 cm) long. Arrange the cinnamon rolls in the prepared pan so they're touching but not too tightly packed. Cover with plastic wrap and a warm towel and let the rolls rise again for 30–45 minutes. They'll puff up and fill the pan beautifully.

9 Preheat your oven to 400°F (200°C). Remove the plastic wrap from your rolls and bake for 20–25 minutes until just slightly golden brown on the edges. You don't want to overbake them; slightly underbaking keeps them soft and gooey in the center. Let cool in the pan for 5–10 minutes while you prepare the frosting.

10 Make the brown butter (see page 14). Melt the butter in a saucepan over medium heat until it foams. Continue to cook, swirling the pan occasionally, until it turns a rich golden brown and releases a nutty aroma. Keep a close eye on it—you don't want it to burn! Remove from the heat and let it cool slightly. In a mixing bowl, beat together the cream cheese and brown butter until smooth and creamy. Gradually beat in the confectioners' sugar until the frosting is thick and spreadable.

11 Generously spread the frosting over the warm cinnamon rolls. The frosting will melt slightly, seeping into all the nooks and crannies of the rolls.

TIP

The dental floss technique for cutting cinnamon rolls is fantastic—it slices through the dough without squishing it, giving you perfect rounds.

Sugar & Spice

Cookies & Cream *Cheesecake Brownies*

Cookies + Cream + Cheesecake—it's already an unbeatable combo. But add it to brownies? WOW. The result is dangerously addictive, with every bite better than the last. Trust me, this is one of those recipes you'll find yourself making again and again (and again).

**Makes 9 large or
16 small squares**

7 oz (200 g) good-quality
   dark chocolate, broken
   into pieces
10 tbsp (150 g) unsalted butter
1 cup (200 g) sugar
2 eggs
Heaped ¾ cup (100 g) all-
   purpose flour
16 cookies and cream cookies
   (I use Oreos), plus extras to
   decorate

For the cheesecake topping
1⅓ cups (300 g) cream cheese
¼ cup (50 g) sugar
Scant ½ cup (100 ml) heavy
   cream
3 tbsp cornstarch
1 tsp vanilla extract

1 Preheat your oven to 400°F (200°C). Line an 8 in (20 cm) square baking pan with parchment paper, leaving overhang on all sides for easy removal.

2 In a large microwave-safe mixing bowl, combine the chocolate and butter. Microwave in 30-second bursts, stirring between each interval, until the butter and chocolate are fully melted and smooth (you can also melt them in a saucepan over low heat, if you prefer).

3 Add the sugar, stirring until combined, then beat in the eggs, one at a time. Sift in the flour, then gently stir together until just combined.

4 Now for the fun part! Pour half of the brownie batter into your prepared pan and smooth it out. Arrange a layer of the cookies over the top, then pour over the remaining batter, carefully smoothing it over the cookies to create an even layer.

5 To make the cheesecake topping, mix together the cream cheese, sugar, heavy cream, cornstarch and vanilla extract in a bowl until smooth. Spread the cheesecake mixture over the brownie batter. For extra crunch and flavor, crush a few more cookies and sprinkle them on top.

6 Bake for about 30 minutes until the edges are slightly firm but the center is still jiggly (they will continue to set as they cool and the middle will firm up when chilled).

7 Remove from the oven and let the brownies cool completely in the pan, then transfer to the fridge to set. For best results, chill the brownies overnight, but if you're short on time, refrigerate for at least 3 hours. When fully chilled, cut into squares and serve.

Earl Grey *Tres Leches Cake*

The ultimate cup of tea, in my opinion, is Earl Grey. When I lived up in Leeds, I wouldn't go a day without having at least three cups—nothing else would do. Now that I'm back in the Midlands, I've scaled down to two, but I'm loyal to Earl Grey, no exceptions. During a trip to New York, I stumbled across tres leches cake, and it's been love ever since. There's something magical about the way these two pair together—the fragrant, slightly citrusy notes of the Earl Grey cut through the richness of the tres leches (three types of milk). It's not overly sweet and the heavy cream on top gives it just the right balance. Absolute perfection.

Makes 12 slices

1 cup (240 ml) milk
4 Earl Grey tea bags
7 tbsp (100 g) unsalted butter, melted
Scant ½ cup (100 ml) vegetable oil
1½ cups (300 g) sugar
4 eggs
2 tsp vanilla extract
3 cups (360 g) self-rising flour
1 tsp baking powder
½ tsp salt

For the Earl Grey leche
⅔ cup (150 ml) canned evaporated milk
⅔ cup (150 ml) sweetened condensed milk
2 Earl Grey teabags

For the cream topping
2½ cups (600 ml) heavy cream
1 tbsp vanilla paste
1 tsp ground cinnamon (optional)

1   Start with the cake layer. Heat the milk in a small saucepan until warm, then remove from the heat and add the tea bags. Let them steep for 10–15 minutes, then discard the tea bags and allow the milk to cool slightly.

2   Preheat your oven to 400°F (200°C). Grease an 8 × 12 in (20 x 30 cm) baking pan and line with parchment paper.

3   In a large bowl, whisk together the melted butter, infused milk, oil and sugar until smooth. Beat in the eggs, one by one, followed by the vanilla. In a separate bowl, sift together the flour, baking powder and salt, then gradually fold in to the wet mixture.

4   Pour the batter into the prepared pan, smooth the top and slightly bang the pan to ensure all the air bubbles are removed. Bake for 20–25 minutes until a toothpick inserted into the center comes out clean.

5   Remove from the oven and let the cake cool slightly, then poke small holes with a fork across the surface to allow the milk mixture to soak in later.

6   To make the Earl Grey leche, heat the evaporated milk and condensed milk in a small saucepan until warm—you should be able to dip your finger in. Remove from the heat, add the tea bags and let them steep for 10 minutes, then discard the tea bags and allow the leche to cool. Pour the mixture over the cake, making sure it seeps into the holes, then refrigerate the cake for at least a couple of hours, or preferably overnight.

7   When ready to serve, make the cream topping. Whip together the cream and vanilla paste in a bowl, then spread or pipe evenly over the top of the cake. Sprinkle with the cinnamon, if desired, and enjoy!

TIP

Due to the amount of milk in this I recommend eating the cake straight away—this won't be hard since it's delicious!

Apple & Pear *Crumble*

I already know this page in the book is destined for chaos—oily fingerprints, smudges, and probably a few stray oats stuck in the crease—because you're all going to LOVE this recipe. Let's be honest, the only way a classic British crumble should be is 30% fruit and 70% crumble. That's the rule, and I won't hear otherwise! The oats add a lovely crunch to the topping, and the sugar gives it a balanced sweetness and a nice golden finish. The fruit will continue to soften slightly as the crumble cools. It's best enjoyed warm, the juices mingling with the buttery, crunchy topping.

Makes 3 hearty servings

Hot custard, to serve

For the filling
2 tart cooking apples, peeled, cored and sliced
2 ripe pears, peeled, cored and sliced
½ cup (100 g) brown sugar
1 tsp ground cinnamon

For the topping
Heaped ¾ cup (100 g) all-purpose flour
7 tbsp (100 g) cold unsalted butter, cubed
½ cup (60 g) rolled oats
2 tbsp brown sugar
¼ cup (50 g) sugar

1　Preheat your oven to 400°F (200°C) and grease an 8 in (20 cm) square or round baking dish.

2　Put all the filling ingredients into a large pot and cook over medium heat for 5–7 minutes, stirring occasionally, until the fruit starts to soften and release its juices (this gentle cooking helps the fruit become tender and juicy and allows the flavors to meld). Transfer the fruit mixture to your prepared baking dish, spreading it out evenly.

3　Now, on to the topping. In a large mixing bowl, combine the flour and butter. Using your fingers and working quickly to keep the butter cold, rub the butter into the flour until the mixture resembles coarse breadcrumbs. Stir in the oats and both sugars until evenly combined.

4　Sprinkle the topping evenly over the fruit, making sure to cover it completely. Don't worry if some areas are uneven; the rustic look adds to the charm of the crumble. Bake for 15–25 minutes until the topping is golden brown and crispy and the fruit filling is bubbling up around the edges. Let the crumble cool for a few minutes before serving with hot custard.

TIP

Hot custard is an absolute MUST with crumble—it's non-negotiable. Look for British custard powder in the international aisle of your supermarket. That said, I do have a soft spot for a scoop of creamy vanilla ice cream melting into the crispy topping. Why not have both? Life's too short to choose!

Classic *Lemon Loaf*

In my eyes, there's nothing quite like a classic lemon loaf cake. While it's always tempting to add a unique twist, sometimes you just can't beat the original. To make this loaf extra special, we're rubbing the lemon zest into the sugar to release the essential oils, giving the cake an irresistibly bright and bold lemon flavor.

Makes 1 loaf

Scant 1 cup (170 g) sugar
    (preferably superfine)
2 unwaxed lemons, finely
    zested
1 lime, finely zested
13 tbsp (185 g) unsalted butter,
    softened, plus extra for
    greasing the pan
1 tsp lemon extract
3 large eggs, at room
    temperature
1½ cups (185 g) all-purpose flour
1 tsp baking powder
⅛ tsp fine salt

For the lemon glaze

1⅓ cups (150 g) confectioners'
    sugar, plus extra
    if needed
1 tsp lemon extract
1 tbsp water

1   Preheat your oven to 400°F (200°C). Grease a 9½ x 5 in (900 g) loaf pan and line with parchment paper, leaving an overhang on all sides for easy removal.

2   Put the sugar and lemon and lime zest into a large mixing bowl, then rub the zest into the sugar using your fingers. This helps release the essential oils from the zest, enhancing the lemony fragrance and flavor of the loaf.

3   Add the butter and lemon extract, then cream together for 3–5 minutes until light and fluffy and the butter is almost white. Whisk in the eggs, one at a time with a tablespoon of the measured flour, ensuring each is fully combined before adding the next. In a separate bowl, sift together the flour and baking powder, add the salt, then gently fold into the wet ingredients, being careful not to overmix.

4   Pour the batter into the prepared loaf pan, spreading it out evenly. Bake for 30–40 minutes until a skewer inserted into the center comes out clean. If needed, cover the top loosely with foil during the last 10 minutes to prevent over-browning.

5   Remove from the oven and let the loaf cool in the pan for 25 minutes, then carefully lift it out using the paper overhang and transfer to a wire rack for at least 2 hours to cool completely.

6   To make the lemon glaze, whisk together all the ingredients in a bowl until smooth and the consistency of glue. If it's too thin, gradually mix in a couple more spoonfuls of confectioners' sugar. If it's too thick, add a teaspoon of water until it reaches the right consistency. Spread the glaze over lemon loaf so it drips over the sides. Slice up and enjoy!

TIP

Make sure to use unwaxed lemons since they have more flavor.

Red Velvet & *White Chocolate Muffins*

These muffins are moist, fluffy and taste just like a classic red velvet cake minus the effort. The butter brings richness, while the oil adds that lovely moisture, and when the vinegar hits the baking powder, it fizzes up like a tiny science experiment—the fizz is the secret behind the soft, velvety crumb of your muffins.

Makes 10 muffins

2 cups (250 g) self-rising flour
¼ cup (20 g) cocoa powder
½ tsp baking soda
10½ oz (300 g) white chocolate, chopped
7 tbsp (100 g) unsalted butter, melted
3½ tbsp vegetable oil
¾ cup (150 g) sugar (preferably superfine)
2 eggs
1 cup (250 ml) buttermilk
1 tsp red food coloring paste
1 tsp baking powder
1 tbsp white wine vinegar

1 Preheat your oven to 400°F (200°C) and line your muffin pans with paper liners, spacing them out in the pans.

2 In a large bowl, sift together the flour, cocoa powder and baking soda. Stir in your white chocolate and set aside.

3 In a separate bowl, whisk together the melted butter and oil until smooth and combined. Add the sugar and whisk until fully dissolved and the mixture is smooth and glossy. Crack in the eggs, one at a time, whisking after each one until the mixture is creamy. Slowly pour in the buttermilk, then stir in the food coloring, making sure you achieve the deep, vibrant red we all know and love. Adjust to your liking, but be careful, a little paste goes a long way.

4 Next, gradually add the flour mixture to your wet mixture. I like to do this in stages, adding about a third at a time. Gently fold together, being very careful not to overwork the batter to keep things light and airy.

5 Now for the fun part! In a separate small bowl, mix together the baking powder and vinegar—it will immediately bubble up, so quickly fold it into your batter until just combined, but do not overmix.

6 Grab a cookie scoop or spoon and evenly divide the mixture among your prepared muffin liners, filling each one about two-thirds full to give them room to rise without overflowing. Bake for 20–25 minutes until a skewer inserted into the centers comes out clean. Let the muffins cool slightly before digging in, but trust me, it's worth the wait!

TIP

Here's a little trick to get those bakery-style muffins with an even rise: place the muffin liners in every other cup, leaving space between each one. This helps air circulate more evenly, giving you muffins with a perfect dome.

Brown Butter *Banana Bread*

I feel like everyone says they make the best banana bread but this honestly is it. There's something magical about the combination of ripe bananas, brown butter and sugar, which creates a rich, nutty, caramel-like flavor that is the backbone of your banana bread. The mini chocolate chips bring just the right amount of sweetness and add little pockets of melty goodness throughout the loaf. The banana sprinkled with sugar on top is also a lovely visual touch and it caramelizes beautifully during baking.

Makes 1 loaf

10 tbsp (150 g) unsalted butter
½ cup (100 g) brown sugar
¼ cup (50 g) sugar
2 eggs
1⅔ cups (200 g) self-rising flour
1 tsp baking soda
Scant 1 cup (150 g) milk chocolate chips
2 very ripe bananas, mashed with 1 tsp cinnamon

For the top
1 banana, halved lengthwise
1 tbsp demerara or coarse brown sugar

1 Let's begin by browning the butter (see page 14). Melt the butter in a small saucepan over medium heat until it starts to foam. Continue to cook, swirling the pan occasionally, until it turns golden brown and releases a lovely nutty aroma. When you see brown bits at the bottom, remove from the heat and let it cool slightly.

2 Preheat your oven to 400°F (200°C) and grease a 9½ x 5 in (900 g) loaf pan or line it with parchment paper.

3 In a large mixing bowl, whisk together both sugars and the brown butter. Now, beat in the eggs, one at a time, and give this a good mix, for 2–3 minutes if using a mixer. In a separate bowl, sift together the flour and baking soda (sifting ensures they are evenly mixed and will help your loaf rise perfectly). Gently fold into the wet mixture, being careful not to overwork the batter. You want to keep it nice and fluffy. Stir in the chocolate chips.

4 Now, for the final (and most important) step: the bananas! Take your mashed bananas and gently fold them into the batter. Pour the batter into your prepared loaf pan, smoothing the top. Place your banana halves gently on top, cut-sides up, then sprinkle with the demerara or coarse brown sugar.

5 Bake for 45–50 minutes until a skewer inserted into the center comes out clean. If the top starts to brown too quickly, loosely cover with foil to prevent the loaf over-browning. Remove from the oven and let it cool in the pan for a few minutes, then transfer to a wire rack to cool completely.

TIP

Patience is key with this one! Waiting until your bananas are really brown is the best way for the banana flavor to come through. Adding the mashed ripe bananas at the end of making your batter ensures that their moisture gets locked in, making your banana bread extra tender and soft.

Vegan Crinkly Top *Brownies*

As you may know, I used to sell brownies and cookies, so I take them very seriously. One thing that always puzzled me was why vegan brownies never seemed to get that signature crinkly top. So, I put on my science hat and figured it out: the key is making sure the sugar is properly dissolved. Nerdy moment over—let's just say these brownies are next-level good. Trust me, you won't miss the eggs or dairy one bit.

Makes 9 large brownies or 16 bite-sized ones

7 oz (200 g) vegan dark chocolate, broken into pieces
10 tbsp (150 g) vegan butter
Scant ½ cup (100 ml) almond milk
1 cup (200 g) sugar (preferably superfine)
1½ cups (175 g) all-purpose flour

1 Preheat your oven to 375°F (190°C) and line an 8 in (20 cm) square baking pan with parchment paper.

2 Melt the chocolate and vegan butter in a heatproof bowl set over a pot of gently bubbling water (a bain-marie), ensuring the bowl doesn't touch the water. Stir occasionally until fully melted and smooth.

3 Set a separate heatproof bowl over the pot of simmering water. Pour in the sugar and almond milk and stir until the sugar fully dissolves and forms a syrup-like consistency. This step is essential for achieving a crinkly top on the brownies.

4 Pour the melted chocolate mixture into the sugar milk syrup over the bain-marie. Using an electric mixer, whisk for 2–3 minutes until it is fully incorporated and the mixture is smooth.

5 Remove the bowl from the bain marie. Add the flour and fold it in until just combined.

6 Pour the batter into the lined pan, spreading it out evenly. Bake for about 25 minutes, or until the top is set and beginning to crack slightly.

7 Remove from the oven and let the brownies cool completely in the pan for at least 3 hours, or preferably overnight in the fridge (this allows the layers to set properly and ensures clean slices when cutting into squares).

TIP

Fudgy brownies take TIME. Chill these in the fridge overnight for ultimate fudgy-ness.

Boozy Mint *Tiramisu*

If you're looking to put a fresh twist on a classic dessert, this boozy mint tiramisu is just the ticket. Let's dive into this layered delight that's sure to impress your guests. A combination of rich coffee and whiskey or rum is used to soak the sponge fingers, infusing them with a rich flavor and a delightful boozy kick, and a hint of peppermint in the luscious, creamy mascarpone makes for a delightful after-dinner treat that's both indulgent and refreshing. The final dusting of cocoa not only adds a rich, chocolatey flavor but also gives your tiramisu that classic, elegant look.

Makes 9 or 18 slices

3 egg yolks
½ cup (110 g) sugar (preferably superfine)
5 tsp peppermint extract (or less depending on strength)
1 tbsp vanilla paste
2½ cups (600 ml) heavy cream
9 oz (250 g) mascarpone cheese
12 oz (350 g) sponge cake fingers or savoiardi/lady fingers (2–2½ packages)
½ oz (15 g) dark chocolate, grated
cocoa powder, for dusting

For the soaking liquid
1⅔ cups (400 ml) boiling water
2 tbsp instant coffee granules
⅓ cup (75 ml) whiskey or dark rum

1 Start by making the soaking liquid for the sponge fingers. Brew a cup of strong coffee with the boiling water and coffee granules, then let it cool to room temperature. When cool, stir in the whiskey or rum and set aside.

2 In a mixing bowl, combine the egg yolks, sugar, peppermint extract and vanilla paste and beat together until lightened in color and fluffy. If using an electric mixer, this will take about 5 minutes.

3 Whip the cream in a separate bowl until soft peaks form (the kind that hold their shape but curl over gently at the tips), but be careful not to over-whip—you want it light and airy. Gently fold in the mascarpone using a spatula and a light hand just until combined, then add your egg yolk mixture and gently fold in.

4 Now comes the fun part! Quickly dip each sponge finger into the coffee and whiskey/rum mixture. Be swift—sponge fingers soak up liquid very quickly! Arrange them snugly in a single layer at the bottom of a 9 × 13 in (23 × 33 cm) serving dish, covering the entire base. Spread half of the mascarpone mixture over the sponge fingers, smoothing it out evenly with your spatula, then sprinkle over a generous amount of the chocolate.

5 Repeat the layering process: another round of soaked sponge fingers, followed by the remaining mascarpone mixture. Smooth out the top layer to make it nice and even. For the finishing touch, dust the top generously with cocoa powder using a fine-mesh sieve.

6 Cover and let it chill for several hours in the fridge—overnight is even better (this allows all those wonderful flavors to meld and gives the tiramisu time to set properly). When you're ready to serve, cut the tiramisu into the desired number of pieces and plate them up.

The Ultimate *Chocolate Chip Cookie*

Yes you read that right; these are the best chewy chocolate chip cookies—it's time to indulge in the sheer delight of brown butter cookies. I tested every ingredient in the recipe to ensure it's perfect, so follow it to a T! The egg yolks add richness and help with that chewy texture.

Makes 12 cookies

8 oz (225 g) unsalted butter, cubed
¾ cup (150 g) sugar (preferably superfine)
⅔ cup (150 g) light brown sugar
⅓ cup (75 ml) cold milk
3 large egg yolks
2¼ cups (270 g) all-purpose flour
1½ tsp baking powder
¾ tsp baking soda
3 tbsp cornstarch
5 oz (150 g) dark chocolate, chopped
5 oz (150 g) milk chocolate, chopped
Sea salt flakes (optional)

1 First, let's brown the butter (see page 14). Melt the butter in a saucepan over medium heat until it starts to foam. Continue to cook, swirling the pan occasionally, until it turns golden brown and releases a nutty aroma. When you see brown bits at the bottom, remove from the heat. Pour into a heatproof bowl and let cool to room temperature (this helps it retain its lovely flavors).

2 Line a baking sheet with parchment paper.

3 Whisk both sugars into the brown butter until smooth and combined, then add the cold milk to further cool down the mixture (this also helps create the right consistency for the dough). Whisk in the egg yolks until they are fully incorporated, then add the flour, baking powder, baking soda and cornstarch and gently stir together until just combined, making sure not to overmix (this can make the cookies tough). Finally, fold in the chocolate until evenly distributed for that perfect chocolatey bite in every cookie, setting aside a handful of chocolate chunks for the top.

4 Press a couple of the reserved chocolate chunks into a cookie scoop, then use the scoop to portion the dough into 12 even-sized balls. Place on the prepared baking sheet, spaced well apart. This ensures a camera-worthy cookie topped with chocolate. Cover and refrigerate overnight.

5 When you're ready to bake, preheat your oven to 400°F (200°C). Remove the cookie dough balls from the fridge and bake for 10–12 minutes until the edges are golden and set but the centers remain slightly soft (they will continue to firm up as they cool).

6 Remove the cookies from the oven and, if they have spread a lot, use a cup to bring in the cookie to a perfect circle shape. Allow to cool on the baking sheet for a few minutes, then transfer to a wire rack to cool completely (if you can wait that long!). Sprinkle with sea salt flakes if you like.

TIP

Chilling your cookie dough before baking is key—it allows the flour to fully hydrate and the flavors to deepen, plus it helps prevent the cookies from spreading too much when baked.

Cherry Bakewell *Blondies*

One of my favorite thing to do is to combine desserts, and these cherry bakewell blondies are the ultimate sweet creation. Picture a frangipane-based blondie with a buttery, chocolatey base that adds a rich flavor and fudgy texture, swirled with a beautiful cherry jam layer and topped with a sprinkle of sliced almonds—perfection in every bite. I'll gladly take three!

Makes 16 slices

12 tbsp (175 g) unsalted butter
5 oz (150 g) white chocolate
⅔ cup (125 g) superfine sugar
Scant ½ cup (75 g) light brown sugar
2 eggs
1 egg yolk
1½ tbsp golden syrup (or light corn syrup)
1 tbsp vanilla paste
1 tsp almond extract
2 cups (250 g) all-purpose flour
1 cup (80 g) ground almonds
¼ cup (25 g) cornstarch
Scant 1 cup (150 g) white chocolate chips

For the topping
½ cup (150 g) cherry jam
⅔ cup (50 g) sliced almonds

1 Preheat your oven to 400°F (200°C) and line an 8 × 12 in (20 x 30 cm) baking pan with parchment paper, leaving an overhang on all sides for easy removal.

2 Melt the butter and chocolate in a saucepan over low heat, then remove from the heat and allow it to cool slightly.

3 In a large mixing bowl, combine both the sugars. Pour in the butter and chocolate mixture and whisk for about 3 minutes, or until well combined and the butter and chocolate are not separated. Add the eggs and egg yolk, one at a time, whisking thoroughly after each addition. Stir in the golden syrup, vanilla paste and almond extract, mixing until they are well incorporated and the batter is smooth and glossy.

4 Sift the flour, ground almonds and cornstarch into the bowl, then gradually fold it into the batter using a spatula until just combined. Gently fold in the chocolate chips, ensuring they're evenly distributed throughout the batter. Pour into your prepared baking pan, spreading it out evenly with a spatula to reach all the corners.

5 Spoon the jam over the top of the batter in small dollops. Using a knife or skewer, gently swirl the jam across the surface, being careful not to swirl too deeply—you want the jam to stay mostly on top. Finally, sprinkle over the sliced almonds.

6 Bake for 20–25 minutes until the blondies are golden around the edges but still slightly soft in the middle.

7 Remove the blondies from the oven and allow them to cool completely in the pan for 2 hours, then refrigerate overnight, or for at least 6 hours (this ensures they set properly and makes slicing easier).

—— TIP

Let's talk about the secret to great blondies: 1. Patience, and 2. The art of 'unbaking." You want to bake these beauties until they're golden around the edges but still wobbly in the center. This is where patience comes in. Let them set in the fridge overnight (or at least 6 hours), and trust me, they'll firm up into chewy, fudgy heaven.

Speculoos Millionaire *Oat Bars*

Although a humble tray bake, I *love* a good oat bar. This recipe takes the classic British flapjack to the next level with layers of rich caramel and a dreamy white chocolate and speculoos topping. The combination of the chewy oats, buttery caramel and sweet topping is absolutely irresistible.

Makes 16 pieces

For the base
2¼ sticks (250 g) unsalted butter
¾ cup (225 g) golden syrup (or light corn syrup)
¼ cup (50 g) sugar
¼ cup (50 g) light brown sugar
2½ tbsp speculoos cookie butter (I use Lotus Biscoff)
1 lb (450 g) oats

For the caramel
7 tbsp (100 g) unsalted butter
2 tbsp speculoos cookie butter (I use Lotus Biscoff)
½ cup (100 g) light brown sugar
2 tbsp golden syrup (or light corn syrup)
14 oz (397 g) can condensed milk

For the topping
9 oz (250 g) white chocolate, broken into pieces
⅓ cup (100 g) speculoos cookie butter (I use Lotus Biscoff)

TIPS

My top tip is to add a tablespoon of oil to the melted chocolate—it helps the chocolate to cut better without snapping. The cut bars can be layered with parchment paper in between to prevent sticking and stored in an airtight container in the fridge for up to 7 days.

1 Preheat your oven to 400°F (200°C). Grease an 8 × 12 in (20 x 30 cm) baking pan and line with parchment paper, leaving an overhang on all sides.

2 Start with the base. Heat the butter, golden syrup, both sugars and speculoos cookie butter in a large pot over medium heat, stirring until the mixture is fully melted and combined. Remove from the heat and stir in the oats, making sure they are evenly coated in the buttery syrup.

3 Transfer the mixture to your prepared baking pan and press it down evenly with the back of a spoon or spatula to form a smooth, even layer. Bake for 15–20 minutes until golden and slightly firm around the edges. Remove from the oven and allow to cool while you prepare the caramel.

4 To make the caramel, melt the butter, speculoos cookie butter, sugar and golden syrup in a saucepan over low heat, stirring until the sugar dissolves and the mixture is combined. Add the condensed milk and bring to a gentle boil, stirring constantly to prevent it burning. Cook for another 5–8 minutes, stirring constantly, until it thickens, turns light golden and is smooth and creamy (it should pull away slightly from the side of the pan when ready). Remove from the heat and let it cool for a minute, then pour evenly over the oat base, using a spatula to smooth it out. Let it set at room temperature or refrigerate to speed up the process.

5 When the caramel has set, make the topping. Melt the chocolate in a heatproof bowl over a pot of gently bubbling water, ensuring the bowl doesn't touch the water (this prevents the chocolate from seizing) or in a microwave-safe bowl in the microwave in short bursts, stirring after each interval, until smooth. Pour over the caramel layer and spread it evenly with a spatula.

6 In a separate bowl, melt the speculoos cookie butter until smooth and pourable, then drizzle over the chocolate. Using a skewer or toothpick, swirl the spread through the chocolate to create a marbled effect.

7 Let the oat bars set in the fridge for at least 1 hour, or until the chocolate is firm, then remove from the pan using the paper overhang and cut into squares or bars.

Charlie's Chocolate & *Speculoos Cake*

I'm a chocolate cake lover through and through, and the moister, the better. This cake is one that would make even Charlie and his chocolate factory jealous. Inspired by @bakedbybenji, this is my take on a chocolate and speculoos cake. Celebration cakes can seem intimidating, but don't worry—I've broken it down into super simple stages. This two-layer cake is a dream come true, combining the richness of chocolate with the unique, caramelized flavor of speculoos. It's filled with a creamy speculoos cookie butter center and topped with a thick, glossy layer of chocolate ganache. Perfect for any celebration—or just because!

Makes 9 slices

2½ oz (75 g) dark chocolate, broken into pieces
7 tbsp (100 g) unsalted butter
1⅔ cups (200 g) all-purpose flour
⅔ cup (60 g) Dutch processed cocoa powder (see Tip on page 223)
2 tsp baking powder
½ tsp baking soda
1¼ cups (250 g) light brown sugar
3 large eggs
3½ tbsp vegetable oil
Scant ½ cup (100 ml) milk
⅔ cup (200 g) speculoos cookie butter (I use Lotus Biscoff), for the filling
2½ tbsp speculoos cookies (I use Lotus), crushed, to decorate

For the chocolate frosting
12 oz (340 g) dark chocolate, broken into pieces
1 stick (120 g) unsalted butter
½ cup (50 g) cocoa powder
1⅔ cups (400 ml) heavy cream
Scant 1 cup (250 g) mascarpone cheese

1 Preheat your oven to 400°F (200°C). Grease two 8 in (20 cm) round cake pans, then line with parchment paper.

2 Start with the cakes. Melt the chocolate and butter together in a heatproof bowl over a pot of gently bubbling water, ensuring the bowl doesn't touch the water (this prevents the chocolate from seizing) or in a microwave-safe bowl in the microwave in 30-second bursts, stirring after each interval, until smooth. Allow to cool slightly.

3 In a large bowl, sift together the flour, cocoa powder, baking powder and baking soda. Stir in the sugar until it is evenly distributed. In a separate bowl, whisk together the eggs, oil and milk until combined, then pour in the chocolate and butter mixture and whisk until smooth. Gradually add the wet mixture to the dry ingredients, stirring gently until just combined, there are no more streaks of flour and the batter is smooth and glossy. Be careful not to overmix.

4 Divide the batter evenly between your prepared cake pans and smooth the tops with a spatula. Bake for 25–30 minutes until a skewer inserted into the centers comes out clean. Remove from the oven and allow to cool in the pans for 10 minutes, then transfer to a wire rack to cool completely.

5 Meanwhile, move on to the chocolate frosting. Melt the chocolate and butter together on the stovetop or in the microwave as in step 2, stirring until smooth. Allow to cool slightly. In a separate bowl, whisk together the cocoa powder and cream until smooth and well combined, then stir in the chocolate mixture until incorporated. Gently fold in the mascarpone until the frosting is creamy and smooth. Refrigerate for 10–15 minutes to firm it up slightly (this makes it easier to spread).

6   When it's time to assemble, place a cake on your serving board or plate. Spread a layer of the chocolate frosting on top, smoothing it out evenly, then pipe a border of the frosting around the edge of the cake.

7   Warm the speculoos cookie butter in a microwave-safe bowl in the microwave for 15–20 seconds until soft and spreadable but not too runny. Spread a thick layer over the frosting, covering the center of the cake. Place the second cake on top, pressing down gently to secure. Refrigerate for 30 minutes to ensure the spread doesn't seep out at the edges.

8   Now, using the remaining frosting, cover the top and sides of the cake. You don't need to be too perfect—rustic looks are just as delicious! Press the crushed cookies around the sides of the cake for added crunch and flavor. When decorated, slice into your decadent cake and enjoy!

Neapolitan *Marble Loaf*

Who remembers chasing down the ice cream truck, begging your parents for some cash, only to hear, "We've got ice cream at home"? And what did you find in the freezer? That budget Neapolitan brick with the uneven layers no one really loved. Well, consider this the ultimate glow-up. This cake takes that humble freezer staple and turns it into a show-stopping cake with a stunning swirl that's bound to impress. It's a serious crowd-pleaser, and trust me—you won't be able to stop at just one slice.

Makes 1 loaf

7 tbsp (100 g) unsalted butter, melted
Scant ½ cup (100 ml) vegetable oil
¾ cup (150 g) sugar (preferably superfine)
2 eggs
1 tbsp vanilla paste
1⅔ cups (200 g) self-rising flour
½ tsp baking powder

For the strawberry batter
2 tbsp milk
Heaped 1 tbsp strawberry custard powder or instant pudding mix
1 tsp pink food coloring

For the chocolate batter
1 tbsp cocoa powder
2 tbsp milk

1   Preheat your oven to 400°F (200°C). Grease a 9½ x 5 in (900 g) loaf pan and line with parchment paper, leaving an overhang on all sides for easy removal.

2   In a large mixing bowl, whisk together the melted butter, oil and sugar until the mixture is smooth and well combined. Add the eggs and vanilla paste and continue to whisk until fully incorporated. In a separate bowl, sift together the flour and baking powder, then fold into the wet mixture and mix until the batter is smooth and just combined, being careful not to overmix (this can make the loaf dense).

3   Divide the batter evenly among 3 clean bowls. Leave one bowl of the mixture aside—this is for your vanilla batter. To make the strawberry batter, add the milk, custard powder and food coloring to the second bowl and mix well until the batter is pink and strawberry-flavored. In the third bowl, fold in the cocoa powder and milk to make the chocolate batter, stirring until the cocoa powder is fully incorporated.

4   Spoon alternating dollops of the vanilla, strawberry and chocolate batters into the prepared loaf pan. You can create a marble effect by swirling the batters together using a knife or skewer, but be careful not to over-swirl; you still want the distinct colors to show through.

5   Bake for 35–45 minutes until a skewer inserted into the center comes out clean, the top is golden brown and the loaf has risen beautifully. Remove from the oven and let the loaf cool in the pan for 10 minutes, then carefully lift it out using the paper overhang and transfer to a wire rack to cool completely.

Triple Chocolate *Muffins*

These muffins are a chocoholic's dream. With rich cocoa powder in the batter and chunks of milk, dark and white chocolate in every bite, they are the ultimate treat.

Makes 8 jumbo muffins

2½ cups (300 g) self-rising flour
1 cup (200 g) sugar
½ cup (50 g) cocoa powder
2 tsp baking powder
1 tsp baking soda
3½ oz (100 g) milk chocolate, chopped
3½ oz (100 g) dark chocolate, chopped
3½ oz (100 g) white chocolate, chopped
5 tbsp (75 g) unsalted butter, melted
5 tbsp (75 ml) vegetable oil
2 eggs
1 cup (250 ml) buttermilk
1 tsp vanilla extract

1   Preheat your oven to 400°F (200°C) and line 2 jumbo muffin pans with paper liners, spacing them out in the pans (see Tip on page 194).

2   In a large mixing bowl, sift together the flour, sugar, cocoa powder, baking powder and baking soda. Give everything a good stir to combine. Add all the chocolate and toss the pieces around in the flour mixture.

3   In a separate bowl, whisk together all the remaining ingredients until smooth and well combined, then pour into the dry ingredients. Using a spatula, gently fold together until just combined. Overmixing makes your muffins tough so a few lumps in the batter are perfectly okay (they help keep the muffins light).

4   Now, fill your muffin liners. For a perfectly sized muffin, aim to fill each liner with 5½ oz (160 g) of batter to ensure they bake evenly and reach that beautiful height we all love. Bake for 20–25 minutes until a skewer inserted into the centers comes out clean.

5   When you remove them from the oven, immediately transfer to a wire rack to cool completely. If left to cool in the pans, the muffins can overcook, which can make them dry.

TIP

My trick of tossing the chopped chocolate in the dry ingredients to give it a flour coating helps prevent the chunks sinking to the bottom of your muffins.

Peach *Cobbler*

Peach cobbler might be more of a hit in the US than the UK, but it's a dessert worth crossing borders for. This version combines tender, juicy peaches with a fluffy, cake-like topping that's taken to the next level with a golden, crunchy sprinkle of sugar. It's simple, comforting, and downright delicious.

Makes 6 large servings

For the peach filling
6 peaches, peeled, pitted and sliced
½ cup (100 g) brown sugar
¼ cup (50 g) white sugar
½ lemon, juiced
1½ tbsp vanilla paste
Pinch of coarse sea salt
1 tsp freshly grated nutmeg
1 tsp ground cinnamon
1 tsp cornstarch

For the cobbler topping
1⅔ cups (200 g) self-rising flour
1¾ oz (50 g) demerara sugar or light brown sugar
¼ cup (50 g) sugar
7 tbsp (100 g) unsalted butter, melted
⅔ cup (150 ml) milk
1 tbsp vanilla paste

1 Preheat your oven to 400°F (200°C) and grease a medium square or round baking dish (about 8 in/20 cm).

2 Begin with the peach filling. Combine the peaches, both sugars and the lemon juice in a large pot, then cook over medium–low heat for 5–7 minutes, stirring occasionally, until the fruit starts to release its juices and soften slightly, but has not turned mushy. Stir in the vanilla paste, salt, nutmeg and cinnamon (the warm spices will bloom in the heat, making the filling even more aromatic). In a small cup, mix the cornstarch with a little water to make a slurry, then pour into the peach mixture and stir gently until it thickens slightly. Remove from the heat and let cool for a few minutes, then spread evenly in your prepared baking dish.

3 Now, for the cobbler topping. Combine the flour and both sugars in a bowl until well mixed. In a separate small bowl, whisk together the melted butter, milk and vanilla paste until smooth, then pour into the dry ingredients, stirring gently until combined.

4 Spoon the batter over the peach filling, covering most of the surface but allowing some of the fruit to peek through for a rustic look. Bake for 40–45 minutes until the topping is golden brown and the peach filling is bubbling around the edges. Let the cobbler cool slightly before serving warm.

TIPS

The baked cobbler will set a little as it cools, but it is best to serve it warm to get that perfect balance of juicy filling and tender topping.

Hazelnut & *Coffee Cake*

Cinnamon, coffee and hazelnut—need I say more? This cake is the perfect cozy treat when you're craving warmth and comfort. Using coffee-infused milk gives it a great depth of flavor and makes it wonderfully moist and flavorful. With its streusel topping and generous layer of crunchy goodness in the middle, everyone will be begging for an extra slice!

Makes 8 slices

3½ tbsp unsalted butter, melted
3½ tbsp vegetable oil
¾ cup (150 g) sugar (preferably superfine)
2 eggs
1 tsp vanilla extract
1 tsp coffee extract (optional)
1½ cups (180 g) self-rising flour
½ tsp baking powder
½ tsp salt
⅓ cup (50 g) whole hazelnuts, roughly chopped

For the coffee milk
½ cup (120 ml) milk
2 tsp instant coffee granules
½ tsp ground cinnamon

For the streusel
½ cup (120 g) demerara sugar or light brown sugar
1⅓ cups (160 g) all-purpose flour
6 tbsp (90 g) unsalted butter, melted
1 tsp ground cinnamon

For the coffee glaze
1 cup (125 g) confectioners' sugar, plus extra if needed
1–2 tbsp brewed coffee

1   First, preheat your oven to 400°F (200°C). Line an 8 in (20 cm) cake pan with parchment paper, then grease.

2   To make the coffee milk, warm up the milk in a small saucepan over low heat—there's no need to bring it to a boil. Stir in the coffee granules and cinnamon until fully dissolved, then let it cool to room temperature.

3   Next, make the streusel. Combine the sugar, flour, melted butter and cinnamon in a small mixing bowl, then using a fork or your fingers, mix together until it forms a crumbly texture (it should hold together when pressed, but easily crumble when you touch it). Set this aside for later.

4   To make the cake, mix together the melted butter, oil and sugar in another bowl until smooth and glossy. Add the eggs, one at a time, beating well after each addition to ensure a light and airy batter. Stir in the vanilla extract and coffee extract, if using, for an extra kick. Pour in the coffee milk, mixing gently to combine. Gradually fold in the flour, baking powder and salt, stirring until just incorporated. Be careful not to overmix—the batter should be smooth, but a few small lumps are perfectly fine.

5   Pour half of the cake batter into your prepared pan, spreading it out evenly with a spatula. Now, sprinkle over half of the streusel mixture and all the hazelnuts, then top with the remaining batter, smoothing it out to cover the streusel completely. Sprinkle the remaining streusel evenly over the top. Bake for 35 minutes until the streusel is golden brown, a skewer inserted into the center comes out clean and the cake has risen beautifully.

Continued overleaf

6   Meanwhile, make the coffee glaze. In a small bowl, combine the confectioners' sugar with the brewed coffee, adding the coffee gradually and stirring until you have a smooth, pourable glaze. If it's too thick, add a little more coffee; if it's too thin, add a touch more confectioners' sugar. The glaze should be just right for drizzling.

7   Remove the cake from the oven and let it cool in the pan for about 15 minutes, then transfer to a wire rack to cool. While the cake is still slightly warm, drizzle the coffee glaze over the top, letting it run down the sides for that rustic, homemade look.

TIP

The streusel will bake into a deliciously crunchy topping for your cake, but only use the hazelnuts to fill the cake—they will burn if you use them on top!

Chocolate & Peanut Butter
Self-Saucing Chocolate Cake

Think Snickers, but in cake form—gooey, luscious and downright irresistible. This chocolate and peanut butter lava cake oozes with rich, molten chocolate and swirls of creamy peanut butter, creating that perfect balance of sweet and salty. It's like digging into the decadent, warm chocolate bar with every spoonful. It might feel a little counterintuitive to pour liquid over your cake batter, but trust the process. As it bakes, the sauce will sink to the bottom, creating a luscious, self-saucing layer that makes this dessert so special.

Serves 8–10

5 tbsp (75 g) salted butter, plus more for greasing
¼ cup (75 g) smooth peanut butter
1½ cups (175 g) self-rising flour
2 tsp baking powder
Scant 1 cup (175 g) sugar
½ cup (50 g) Dutch processed cocoa powder
3 large eggs
⅔ cup (150 ml) milk
Heaped ½ cup (100 g) milk chocolate chips
½ cup (65 g) roasted nuts, roughly chopped (I used a mixture of peanuts and cashews)
Whipped cream or ice cream, to serve

For the sauce
3 tbsp smooth peanut butter
½ cup (100 g) light brown sugar
1 cup (250 ml) boiling water

1 Preheat your oven to 375°F (190°C) and generously grease a deep 9 × 13 in (23 × 33 cm) baking dish with some of the butter.

2 Melt the butter and the peanut butter in a saucepan over low heat, stirring gently until smooth and creamy. Leave to cool slightly.

3 In a large mixing bowl, mix together the flour, baking powder, sugar and cocoa powder, then give it a quick whisk to ensure everything is well combined. In a separate bowl, whisk the eggs and milk until thoroughly mixed. Gradually pour in the butter and peanut butter mixture, whisking continuously (this helps prevent the eggs cooking in any residual heat from the melted butter).

4 Create a well in the center of your dry ingredients, then pour the wet mixture into the well, stirring gently with a spatula or wooden spoon. Mix until just combined. Fold in the chocolate and nuts. Pour the batter into your prepared baking dish, smoothing the top with your spatula to ensure even baking.

Continued overleaf

5 Now comes the magical part—the sauce that will form underneath the cake as it bakes. In a heatproof bowl, combine the peanut butter and sugar. Gradually whisk in the boiling water, stirring until the sugar dissolves and you have a smooth, thin sauce, then gently pour over the cake batter.

6 Bake for 30 minutes, or until the top of the cake is firm to the touch, the sauce is bubbling up around the edges and a skewer inserted into the center of the cake comes out clean. Allow to stand for a few minutes before serving (this lets the sauce thicken slightly and makes serving easier), then scoop generously into individual bowls, making sure to dig deep and get plenty of that decadent sauce from the bottom. Serve with whiped cream or ice cream.

TIP

Dutch processed cocoa powder adds another level of decadence to this dessert, but regular cocoa powder works just fine. Greasing your baking dish ensures your cake doesn't stick and makes serving a breeze.

Sugar & Spice

Carrot Cake *Cheesecake*

Let's be honest—the real star of a carrot cake is always the cream cheese frosting. So, I thought, why not take it a step further and create a cream-cheese cheesecake with chunks of carrot cake mixed in? To keep things super easy, this recipe is entirely no-bake and uses ready-made carrot cake. It's perfect for when you want to impress guests without any hassle.

Makes 16 slices

For the base
6 oz (175 g) ginger cookies
5 tbsp (75 g) unsalted butter, melted

For the filling
1¼ cups (300 ml) very cold heavy cream
10½ oz (300 g) white chocolate, broken into pieces
1¾ cups (400 g) full-fat cream cheese, at room temperature
7 oz (200 g) pre-made carrot cake, crumbled into bite-sized chunks
½ cup (50 g) chopped walnuts
½ tsp ground cinnamon

To decorate
⅔ cup (200 g) speculoos cookie butter (I use Lotus Biscoff)
Generous ¾ cup (200 ml) heavy cream, whipped (optional)

1 Start by preparing the base. Crush the ginger cookies into fine crumbs, then transfer to a mixing bowl and pour in the melted butter. Mix together until the mixture resembles wet sand, then press firmly into the bottom of an 8 in (20 cm) round cake pan, using the back of a spoon to smooth it out. Put in the fridge to chill while you move on to the filling.

2 In a large bowl, whip the cream until soft peaks form, being careful not to over-whip—it should stay light and fluffy.

3 Melt the white chocolate in a heatproof bowl set over a pot of gently bubbling water, ensuring the bowl doesn't touch the water (this prevents the chocolate from seizing). Stir the chocolate gently until fully melted and smooth, then let it cool for a few minutes.

4 Put the cream cheese into another large bowl and pour in the chocolate, mixing until smooth and well combined. Gently fold this mixture into the whipped cream. Fold in the carrot cake pieces, walnuts and cinnamon, then spread evenly over the chilled cookie base.

5 Melt the speculoos cookie butter in a microwave-safe bowl or in a saucepan until it becomes smooth and pourable, then carefully spread it over the top of the cheesecake. Refrigerate for at least 4 hours, or ideally overnight, until completely set. When you are ready to serve, pipe swirls of whipped cream on top (if using).

Pistachio Skillet *Cookie*

What's your favorite part of a cookie—the gooey center or the crispy outer edge? For me, it's all about that crispy edge, while my friends are all about the gooey middle. That's what makes a skillet cookie so perfect! You get a big, crispy outer layer, and the deeper you go, the gooier it gets. It's the ultimate crowd-pleaser and ideal for hosting. Plus, it's a one-pan wonder: just mix everything in one bowl, press it back into the skillet, bake and you're done.

Makes 4–6 hearty portions

2 sticks (225 g) salted butter
¾ cup (150 g) sugar
⅔ cup (150 g) light brown sugar
2 eggs
3 cups (350 g) all-purpose flour
1½ tsp baking powder
¾ tsp baking soda
1¼ cups (150 g) pistachios, roughly chopped
5 oz (150 g) dark chocolate, roughly chopped

1   Preheat your oven to 400°F (200°C).

2   Start by browning the butter (see page 14). Melt the butter in an ovenproof skillet over medium heat until it starts to foam. Continue to cook, stirring continuously, until it turns golden brown and releases a nutty aroma. Keep a close eye on it—you don't want it to burn! Carefully pour the butter into a large mixing bowl and let it cool slightly. Set aside the skillet.

3   Add both the sugars to the cooled butter, whisking until smooth and well combined. Add the eggs, one at a time, mixing well after each addition. Stir in the flour, baking powder and baking soda until they are just combined. Finally, fold in the pistachios and chocolate until evenly distributed, but avoid overmixing or the warm butter will make the chocolate melt.

4   Transfer the dough to the skillet, pressing it into an even layer. Bake for 20–25 minutes until the edges are golden and the center is just set. Allow to cool slightly before digging in—enjoy it warm and gooey!

TIP

I recommend using a cast-iron skillet for this cookie—it makes the bottom and edges super crispy, which are my fave part!

INDEX

A

air fryer chocolate sprinkle doughnuts 168
air fryer cinnamon bites 150
almonds
    almond croissant cookies 146
    cherry bakewell blondies 204
apple & pear crumble 190
avocados
    carne asada tacos 96

B

baking tips 16–19
bananas
    banana bread cinnamon rolls 182–5
    brown butter banana bread 196
    caramelized banana French toast 152
    malted milk banana pudding 154
bean sprouts
    beef chow mein 106
béchamel sauce
    Italian sausage lasagna 24–6
    macaroni béchamel 50
beef
    beef chow mein 106
    beef patties 54–7
    braised beef short ribs with Stilton mash 42
    carne asada tacos 96
    chile cheeseburgers 88
    Italian sausage lasagna 24–6
    macaroni béchamel 50
    Mom's best jollof rice 114
    okra soup 128
    Queeny's meat pies 132–5
    yam & egusi stew 124
beer
    carne asada tacos 96
biscuits. see cookies
blondies
    cherry bakewell blondies 204
blueberries
    blueberry & rosemary muffins 174
    cream cheese & blueberry doughnuts 166
    lemon & blueberry streusel cake 178
bofrot
    puff puff (bofrot) 110
boozy mint tiramisu 201
braised beef short ribs with Stilton mash 42

brown butter. see butter
brown stew chicken 49
brownies
    cookies & cream cheesecake brownies 186
    single serve brownie pie 138
    vegan crinkly top brownies 198
burger sauce
    chile cheeseburgers 88
burgers
    chile cheeseburgers 88
    golden arches fish 68
butter 14
    brown butter banana bread 196
    brown butter crispy treats 173
    gochujang chicken Kyiv 31
butter chicken 75
buttermilk
    Mr. American fried chicken 64
    red velvet & white chocolate muffins 194

C

Cajun wedges 101
cakes
    air fryer chocolate sprinkle doughnuts 168
    banana bread cinnamon rolls 182–5
    blueberry & rosemary muffins 174
    brown butter banana bread 196
    Charlie's chocolate & speculoos cake 208–9
    cherry bakewell blondies 204
    classic lemon loaf 193
    cookies & cream cheesecake brownies 186
    cookies & cream mug cake 142
    cream cheese & blueberry doughnuts 166
    Earl Grey tres leches cake 188
    hazelnut & coffee cake 219–20
    lemon & blueberry streusel cake 178
    Neapolitan marble loaf 212
    red velvet & white chocolate muffins 194
    single serve brownie pie 138
    single serve cinnamon roll 141
    speculoos millionaire oat bars 206
    sticky toffee pudding loaf with miso caramel 180
    triple chocolate muffins 214
    vegan crinkly top brownies 198
caramel
    everything-but cookies 160–1

speculoos millionaire oat bars 206
sticky toffee pudding loaf with miso caramel 180
caramelized banana French toast 152
cardamom 13
carne asada tacos 96
carrots
carrot cake cheesecake 225
sweet & sour paneer 102
cauliflower
Korean fried "Chkn" wings 94
char siu BBQ pork 71
Charlie's chocolate & speculoos cake 208–9
Cheddar
honey jalapeño cornbread 58
Italian sausage lasagna 24–6
macaroni béchamel 50
three-cheese mac & cheese 52
cheeky lemon & herb chicken 72
cherry bakewell blondies 204
chicken
brown stew chicken 49
butter chicken 75
cheeky lemon & herb chicken 72
chicken kebabs with saffron rice 79–80
chipotle cream enchiladas 46
gochujang chicken Kyiv 31
groundnut soup 120
happy it's Friday sesame chicken bites 82
mango habanero wings 87
Mr. American fried chicken 64
roast chicken with rosemary salt potatoes & salsa verde 38–9
suya chicken 116
chicken bouillon powder 13
chiles
cheeky lemon & herb chicken 72
chile cheeseburgers 88
mango habanero wings 87
salt & pepper fries 66
shito (West African chile oil) 131
spicy tofu saag 78
chipotle cream enchiladas 46
chocolate
air fryer chocolate sprinkle doughnuts 168
brown butter banana bread 196
carrot cake cheesecake 225
Charlie's chocolate & speculoos cake 208–9
cherry bakewell blondies 204
chocolate & peanut butter self-saucing chocolate cake 221–3
chocolate chip air fryer cookies 156
cookies & cream cheesecake brownies 186
cookies & cream mug cake 142

emergency dessert chocolate mousse 170
everything-but cookies 160–1
honeycomb & caramelized chocolate cookies 162
pistachio skillet cookie 226
raspberry & white chocolate cookies 157
red velvet & white chocolate muffins 194
single serve brownie pie 138
triple chocolate muffins 214
the ultimate chocolate chip cookie 202
ultimate speculoos white hot chocolate 165
vegan crinkly top brownies 198
chow mein sauce
beef chow mein 106
cilantro rice 74
cinnamon 13
air fryer cinnamon bites 150
banana bread cinnamon rolls 182–5
single serve cinnamon roll 141
classic lemon loaf 193
coconut cream
jerk mushroom pasta 60
cod
golden arches fish 68
coffee
boozy mint tiramisu 201
hazelnut & coffee cake 219–20
cookies
almond croissant cookies 146
chocolate chip air fryer cookies 156
everything-but cookies 160–1
honeycomb & caramelized chocolate cookies 162
pistachio skillet cookie 226
raspberry & white chocolate cookies 157
the ultimate chocolate chip cookie 202
cookies & cream cheesecake brownies 186
cookies & cream mug cake 142
cornbread
honey jalapeño cornbread 58
corned beef & egg stew 119
crayfish
shito (West African chile oil) 131
yam & egusi stew 124
cream
air fryer chocolate sprinkle doughnuts 168
boozy mint tiramisu 201
caramelized banana French toast 152
carrot cake cheesecake 225
Charlie's chocolate & speculoos cake 208–9
chipotle cream enchiladas 46
cookies & cream cheesecake brownies 186
Earl Grey tres leches cake 188

emergency dessert chocolate mousse 170
malted milk banana pudding 154
no-churn strawberry cheesecake ice cream 149
spicy burnt sausage pasta 44
spicy tofu saag 78
sticky toffee pudding loaf with miso caramel 180
ultimate speculoos white hot chocolate 165
vodka & 'nduja rigatoni 34
cream cheese
   banana bread cinnamon rolls 182–5
   carrot cake cheesecake 225
   cookies & cream cheesecake brownies 186
   cream cheese & blueberry doughnuts 166
crumbles
   apple & pear crumble 190
   single serve strawberry crisp 144
cumin seeds 13
curried mutton pot pie 28
curry sauce
   butter chicken 75

D

dates
   sticky toffee pudding loaf with miso caramel 180
desserts
   apple & pear crumble 190
   boozy mint tiramisu 201
   caramelized banana French toast 152
   carrot cake cheesecake 225
   chocolate & peanut butter self-saucing
     chocolate cake 221–3
   emergency dessert chocolate mousse 170
   malted milk banana pudding 154
   no-churn strawberry cheesecake ice cream 149
   peach cobbler 216
   pistachio skillet cookie 226
   single serve strawberry crisp 144
   sticky toffee pudding loaf with miso caramel 180
doughnuts
   air fryer chocolate sprinkle doughnuts 168
   cream cheese & blueberry doughnuts 166
drinks
   ultimate speculoos white hot chocolate 165

E

Earl Grey tres leches cake 188
eggs
   corned beef & egg stew 119
   kimchi fried rice 104
egusi
   yam & egusi stew 124

emergency dessert chocolate mousse 170
enchiladas
   chipotle cream enchiladas 46
everything-but cookies 160–1

F

fish
   golden arches fish 68
frying pan spicy pepperoni pizza 90–3

G

garlic granules 13
garlic Parmesan fries 84
glazes
   happy it's Friday sesame chicken bites 82
gochujang paste
   gochujang chicken Kyiv 31
   kimchi fried rice 104
   Korean fried "Chkn" wings 94
golden arches fish 68
groundnut soup 120
guacamole
   carne asada tacos 96

H

happy it's Friday sesame chicken bites 82
harissa paste
   spaghetti & lamb harissa meatballs 36
hazelnut & coffee cake 219–20
herbs
   cheeky lemon & herb chicken 72
   roast chicken with rosemary salt potatoes &
     salsa verde 38–9
honey jalapeño cornbread 58
honeycomb & caramelized chocolate cookies 162

I

ice cream
   no-churn strawberry cheesecake ice cream 149
ingredients, measuring 18
Italian sausage lasagna 24–6

J

jalapeño chiles
   honey jalapeño cornbread 58
jerk mushroom pasta 60
jollof rice
   Mom's best jollof rice 114

K

Kashmiri chile powder 13
kebabs
    chicken kebabs with saffron rice 79–80
kimchi fried rice 104
Korean fried "Chkn" wings 94

L

lamb
    spaghetti & lamb harissa meatballs 36
lasagna
    Italian sausage lasagna 24–6
lemons
    carne asada tacos 96
    cheeky lemon & herb chicken 72
    classic lemon loaf 193
    lemon & blueberry streusel cake 178

M

macaroni
    macaroni béchamel 50
    three-cheese mac & cheese 52
malted milk banana pudding 154
mango habanero wings 87
marshmallows
    brown butter crispy treats 173
mascarpone
    boozy mint tiramisu 201
    Charlie's chocolate & speculoos cake 208–9
measuring ingredients 18
meatballs
    spaghetti & lamb harissa meatballs 36
milk
    Earl Grey tres leches cake 188
    ultimate speculoos white hot chocolate 165
Mom's best jollof rice 114
mousse
    emergency dessert chocolate mousse 170
mozzarella
    chipotle cream enchiladas 46
    frying pan spicy pepperoni pizza 90–3
    Italian sausage lasagna 24–6
    not-birria tacos 32
    three-cheese mac & cheese 52
Mr. American fried chicken 64
mushrooms
    jerk mushroom pasta 60
mutton
    curried mutton pot pie 28

N

'nduja paste 34
Neapolitan marble loaf 212
no-churn strawberry cheesecake ice cream 149
noodles
    beef chow mein 106
not-birria tacos 32
nutmeg 13

O

oats
    apple & pear crumble 190
    single serve strawberry crisp 144
    speculoos millionaire oat bars 206
oil
    shito (West African chile oil) 131
okra soup 128
onion chutney
    cheesy caramelized onion rolls 98
onion granules 13
onions 12
    frying pan spicy pepperoni pizza 90–3
    kimchi fried rice 104
    salt & pepper fries 66
oranges
    carne asada tacos 96
Oreos
    cookies & cream cheesecake brownies 186
    cookies & cream mug cake 142
oven temperature 17

P

paneer
    sweet & sour paneer 102
pans, size of 19
paprika, smoked 13
Parmesan
    garlic Parmesan fries 84
    jerk mushroom pasta 60
    spicy burnt sausage pasta 44
    vodka & 'nduja rigatoni 34
pasta
    Italian sausage lasagna 24–6
    jerk mushroom pasta 60
    macaroni béchamel 50
    spaghetti & lamb harissa meatballs 36
    spicy burnt sausage pasta 44
    three-cheese mac & cheese 52
    vodka & 'nduja rigatoni 34

peach cobbler 216
peanut butter
   chocolate & peanut butter self-saucing
     chocolate cake 221–3
   everything-but cookies 160–1
   groundnut soup 120
pears
   apple & pear crumble 190
pepperoni
   frying pan spicy pepperoni pizza 90–3
peppers
   beef chow mein 106
   brown stew chicken 49
   jerk mushroom pasta 60
   mango habanero wings 87
   not-birria tacos 32
   sweet & sour paneer 102
   yam porridge 130
pies & pastries
   beef patties 54–7
   cheesy caramelized onion rolls 98
   curried mutton pot pie 28
   Queeny's meat pies 132–5
pineapple
   sweet & sour paneer 102
pistachio skillet cookie 226
pizzas
   frying pan spicy pepperoni pizza 90–3
pork
   char siu BBQ pork 71
   Italian sausage lasagna 24–6
   not-birria tacos 32
potatoes
   braised beef short ribs with Stilton mash 42
   Cajun wedges 101
   garlic Parmesan fries 84
   roast chicken with rosemary salt potatoes
     & salsa verde 38–9
   salt & pepper fries 66
pretzels
   everything-but cookies 160–1
puff puff (bofrot) 110
puffed rice
   brown butter crispy treats 173

Q

Queeny's meat pies 132–5

R

raspberry & white chocolate cookies 157
Red Leicester
   cheesy caramelized onion rolls 98
   honey jalapeño cornbread 58
   Italian sausage lasagna 24–6
   three-cheese mac & cheese 52
red velvet & white chocolate muffins 194
ribs
   braised beef short ribs with Stilton mash 42
rice
   chicken kebabs with saffron rice 79–80
   cilantro rice 74
   kimchi fried rice 104
   Mom's best jollof rice 114
   sweet & sour paneer 102
   West African fried rice 122
rigatoni
   vodka & 'nduja rigatoni 34
roast chicken with rosemary salt potatoes & salsa
 verde 38–9
rolls
   banana bread cinnamon rolls 182–5
rosemary syrup
   blueberry & rosemary muffins 174

S

saag sauce
   spicy tofu saag 78
saffron
   chicken kebabs with saffron rice 79–80
salsa verde
   roast chicken with rosemary salt potatoes &
     salsa verde 38–9
salt & pepper fries 66
sausages
   cheesy caramelized onion rolls 98
   spicy burnt sausage pasta 44
   West African fried rice 122
sesame seeds
   happy it's Friday sesame chicken bites 82
   Korean fried "Chkn" wings 94
shito (West African chile oil) 131
shrimp
   shito (West African chile oil) 131
   West African fried rice 122
single serve brownie pie 138
single serve cinnamon roll 141
single serve strawberry crisp 144
soup
   groundnut soup 120
   okra soup 128

spaghetti & lamb harissa meatballs 36
spam
  kimchi fried rice 104
speculoos cookie butter
  carrot cake cheesecake 225
  Charlie's chocolate & speculoos cake 208–9
  speculoos millionaire oat bars 206
  ultimate speculoos white hot chocolate 165
spices 13
spicy burnt sausage pasta 44
spicy tofu saag 78
spinach
  spicy tofu saag 78
sticky toffee pudding loaf with miso caramel 180
Stilton
  braised beef short ribs with Stilton mash 42
strawberries
  no-churn strawberry cheesecake ice cream 149
  single serve strawberry crisp 144
suya chicken 116
sweet & sour paneer 102

T

tacos
  carne asada tacos 96
  not-birria tacos 32
tartar sauce
  golden arches fish 68
three-cheese mac & cheese 52
tiramisu
  boozy mint tiramisu 201
toast
  caramelized banana French toast 152
tofu
  spicy tofu saag 78
tomatoes
  corned beef & egg stew 119
  frying pan spicy pepperoni pizza 90–3
  macaroni béchamel 50
  Mom's best jollof rice 114
  spaghetti & lamb harissa meatballs 36
tortillas
  carne asada tacos 96
  chipotle cream enchiladas 46
  not-birria tacos 32
triple chocolate muffins 214
turkey
  groundnut soup 120

U

ugwu leaves
  yam & egusi stew 124
the ultimate chocolate chip cookie 202
ultimate speculoos white hot chocolate 165

V

vegan crinkly top brownies 198
vegetables
  Queeny's meat pies 132–5
  West African fried rice 122
vodka & 'nduja rigatoni 34

W

walnuts
  carrot cake cheesecake 225
West African fried rice 122

Y

yam
  yam & egusi stew 124
  yam porridge 130
yogurt
  cheeky lemon & herb chicken 72
  chicken kebabs with saffron rice 79–80

Sugar & Spice

CONVERSION TABLES

Recipes have been tested using metric measurements and imperial conversions may yield different results. Follow one set of measurements only—do not mix metric and imperial.

WEIGHTS	
Metric	**Imperial**
15 g	½ oz
25 g	1 oz
40 g	1½ oz
50 g	2 oz
75 g	3 oz
100 g	4 oz
150 g	5 oz
175 g	6 oz
200 g	7 oz
225 g	8 oz
250 g	9 oz
275 g	10 oz
350 g	12 oz
375 g	13 oz
400 g	14 oz
425 g	15 oz
450 g	1 lb
550 g	1¼ lb
675 g	1½ lb
900 g	2 lb
1.5 kg	3 lb
1.75 kg	4 lb
2.25 kg	5 lb

VOLUME	
Metric	**Imperial**
5 ml	1 tsp
15 ml	1 tbsp
60 ml	¼ cup
80 ml	⅓ cup
120 ml	½ cup
150 ml	⅔ cup
180 ml	¾ cup
240 ml	1 cup
480 ml	2 cups
700 ml	3 cups
1 liter	4¼ cups (1 quart)
1.25 liters	5¼ cups
1.5 liters	6⅓ cups
1.6 liters	6¾ cups
1.75 liters	7⅓ cups
1.8 liters	7⅔ cups
2 liters	8½ cups (2 quarts)
2.1 liters	9 cups
2.25 liters	9½ cups
2.5 liters	10½ cup
2.8 liters	12 cups (3 quarts)
3.5 liters	15 cups
3.8 liters	16 cups (1 gallon)

MEASUREMENTS

Metric	Imperial	Metric	Imperial
0.5 cm	¼ inch	23 cm	9 inches
1 cm	½ inch	25 cm	10 inches
2.5 cm	1 inch	30 cm	12 inches
5 cm	2 inches		
7.5 cm	3 inches		
10 cm	4 inches		
15 cm	6 inches		
18 cm	7 inches		
20 cm	8 inches		

OVEN TEMPERATURES

°C	Fan °C	°F	Gas Mark
140°C	120°C	275°F	Gas Mark 1
150°C	130°C	300°F	Gas Mark 2
160°C	140°C	325°F	Gas Mark 3
180°C	160°C	350°F	Gas Mark 4
190°C	170°C	375°F	Gas Mark 5
200°C	180°C	400°F	Gas Mark 6
220°C	200°C	425°F	Gas Mark 7
230°C	210°C	450°F	Gas Mark 8
240°C	220°C	475°F	Gas Mark 9

ACKNOWLEDGMENTS

Creating this cookbook has been a whirlwind of a journey, one filled with love, laughter, the occasional kitchen disaster and, of course, loads of tears. It has been a labor of love, remembering and recreating cherished family recipes, creating and improving fan favorites and putting my stamp on flavorful desserts. I am deeply grateful for the role food has played in my life—bringing people together, sparking connections and telling stories without words.

First and foremost, I want to thank my family. Mama, thank you for instilling in me an early love of cooking and for sharing your invaluable culinary wisdom. You taught me that food is not merely nourishment; it's an expression of love. Papa, your unwavering work ethic and perfectionism have shaped me profoundly. Without your example and encouragement this book might still be a dream. Working two jobs for two and a half years gave me the motivation and determination to bring this project to life, and I owe that drive to you.

To my siblings, my **best** friends: your contributions have been immeasurable. Queeny, your incredible meat pie recipe is a cornerstone of this book and I'll always treasure the cooking lessons you've shared with me. Funmi, your infectious joy and creative energy have been a constant source of inspiration. Thank you for reminding me to embrace the fun and spontaneity of the kitchen, even during the busiest moments. And Bunmi, thank you for being my anchor and reminding me, in the simplest and kindest ways, that I'm just a girl pursuing her passion.

To my fiancé Liam: your steadfast support, boundless patience, late night FaceTimes and enthusiastic taste-testing (even when you thought you were all caked out) have been the backbone of this project. Your love for my Golden Arches Fish will always bring a smile to my face and a sense of warmth to this journey. Thank you for cheering me on **every** step of the way.

To my friends and recipe testers: Tanita, Eisa, Maryam, Anjgy, Gary, Debbie, Mia, Paula and Neil. Thank you for your unwavering encouragement and invaluable feedback. You embraced eating all my experiments with open arms and honest critiques, helping me refine these recipes to something truly special. Sharing this process with you has been an absolute joy.

This cookbook would not have been possible without the contributions of so many talented individuals. To my editors, food stylists and photographer, your expertise and vision have brought this book to life in ways I could only imagine. To my publisher and everyone involved in the process, thank you for believing in this project and guiding me every step of the way.

To you, the readers, thank you for welcoming these recipes into your homes and kitchens. I hope that this cookbook brings you as much joy as it brought me creating it. Whether you're preparing an old favorite or trying something new, I hope these pages inspire laughter, togetherness, and maybe even a new tradition or two. Please share your creations and stories—I would love to hear how these recipes become part of your lives.

Reflecting on this, I am truly overwhelmed with gratitude. This cookbook is more than just a collection of recipes; it celebrates the connections we build through food. To everyone who has been a part of this journey, thank you from the bottom of my heart. You have made this dream possible.

First published in 2025 by

Interlink Books
An imprint of Interlink Publishing Group, Inc.
46 Crosby Street
Northampton, Massachusetts 01060
www.interlinkbooks.com

Published simultaneously in the United Kingdom
by Ebury Press, part of the Penguin Random House
group of companies.

Library of Congress Cataloging-in-Publication Data available
ISBN 978-1-62371-586-1

Editorial Director: Sam Crisp
Senior Editor: Emily Brickell
American Edition Editor: Leyla Moushabeck
Production Manager: Phil Spencer
Designer: Olivia Bush, Studio Nic&Lou
Photographer: Mowie Kay
Food Stylists: Sonali Shah and Kristine Jakobsson
Prop Stylist: Libby Silbermann

Color origination by Altaimage Ltd
Printed and bound in Germany by MOHN Media

Interlink Publishing Group, Inc. is committed to a sustainable future for our business, our readers and our planet. This book is made from Forest Stewardship Council® certified paper.